I.

INTRODUCTION

The newly arrived Army Judge Advocate officer in Viet-Nam read through the two war crimes files assigned to him to prosecute as capital offenses before US military tribunals. The offenses had taken place in South Viet-Namese territory during the time of US military assistance to defend against the armed aggression from North Viet-Nam.[1] The first file concerned the murder of a village chief, his wife and three children, and two teachers by two members of the North Viet-Nam Army.[2] The second file reflected that a US Army batallion commander had been fatally shot in his sleep by three guerrillas who had posed as indigenous mess hall employees, thereby gaining admission to the compound early one morning and thereafter

---

1.   The explanation of the Administration's policy of assistance and the recognition in international law of self-defense in the face of armed aggression is outlined by the Legal Advisor to the State Department, Mr. Meeker, in The Legality of United States Participation in the Defense of Viet-Nam, 54 State Dept Bull. 474, 28 March 1966; see also Meeker, Viet-Nam and International Law of Self-Defense, 56 State Dept Bull. 56 (1967); Rusk, Viet-Nam: Four Steps to Peace, 53 State Dept Bull. 50 (12 July 1965). See also Q Wright, Legal Aspects of the Viet-Nam Situation, 60 Am. J. Int'l. L. J 750 (1966) and for criticism of the U.S. position, see Falk, International Law and the United States Role in the Viet Nam War, 75 Yale L. J. 1122 (1966).

2.   A brief summary of the violence inflicted upon helpless civilians in South Viet Nam, including mining of roads, kidnapping villagers, burning homes, and torture and murder of governmental officials and their families, see Mallin, TERROR IN VIET NAM (1966). President Johnson reports that in 1965, the Viet Cong killed or kidnapped 12,000 South Vietnamese civilians, 55 State Dept Bull 144, 117 (1966).

entering the victim's tent where he slept.[3] The files contained
both sworn and unsworn statements from witnesses, mostly regarding
hearsay matters; depositions from several villagers and from some
US military personnel who had been reassigned to either the US or
Europe or had been discharged; and sworn statements from the four
accused in custody which the CID, in cooperation with the Viet-
Namese authorities, had obtained. The fifth accused, one of the
guerrillas, had fled to a neighboring state. The trials had been
authorized by higher headquarters and qualified US Army counsel had
been assigned to represent the five defendants and interpreters
provided to each accused or his counsel.

The Army prosecutor leaned back in his chair, gazed at the
overhead fan stirring the humid air, and considered the procedural
aspects of these trials: What duty, if any, does the United States
have regarding a fair trial under international law? If such a
duty exists, what are the components of a "fair trial"? To what
extent does the 1949 Geneva Conventions affect the conduct of a war
crimes trial? Upon what principles of jurisdiction can the trials
be conducted? Can the accused have a choice of defense counsel and,
if so, what qualifications must he possess? What about the right of
the accused to call witnesses and present evidence, and can the
statements and depositions be introduced? Does international law

---

3.   Kelly, Assassination in War Time, 30 Mil L Rev 101 (1966);
Baxter, So-Called 'Unprivileged Belligerency: Spies, Guerrillas,
and Saboteurs, 28 Brit. Yb. Int'l. L. 323, 342-3 (1951). See also
COMMENTARY III, infra note 37 at 61.

permit trial in absentia? What punishment is imposable in the event of conviction? And, finally, what judicial and non-judicial remedies are available to assert a claim of denial of justice?

The present inquiry deals with the procedural aspects of the general topic of state responsibility arising from the prosecution of violations of the law of war during hostilities as well as occupation and will be considered under the following headings: standards of due process of law under international law, principles of jurisdiction, types of war crimes tribunals, procedural rights accorded a prisoner of war and the unlawful belligerent (guerrilla) for offenses committed during hostilities and during occupation, procedural rights granted in the trial of a grave breach, and post-trial actions regarding such proceedings.

The paper is restricted, so far as possible, to the problem of the trial of the enemy alien conducted outside the US and the impact of customary international law and the 1949 Geneva Conventions upon war crimes trials. Emphasis is upon the prosecution of conventional war crimes and grave breaches[4] against prisoners of war

---

4.   War crimes are generally divided into three categories: a) crimes against peace - the planning, preparation, initiation or waging of a war of aggression; b) crimes against humanity - deportation, enslavement and other inhuman acts committed against large populations; and c) war crimes - violations against the laws of war - murder, ill-treatment or deportation of slave labor of civilian populations, killing of hostages, plunder, and wanton destruction of villages, towns and cities. Stone, LEGAL CONTROLS OF INTERNATIONAL CONFLICT 358 (1954). The term 'grave breaches' combines the more serious crimes from the categories of conventional war crimes and crimes against humanity. Little has been asserted as to the war

and unlawful belligerents before US Army tribunals. The paper does not deal, except quite incidentally, with what constituted a war crime or with other substantive or evidentiary matters.

It is not the purpose of this paper to advocate in any way that war crimes trials be conducted by the US, but merely to review critically the WW II war crimes trials conducted by the US and to analyze the provisions of the Geneva Conventions in order to determine what action the United States Army must or should follow in the event it is assigned the task of conducting such trials.

---

against peace as being a valid substantive war crime. See II Oppenheim, INTERNATIONAL LAW 566-7, (7th ed, 1952) for the inclusion of all marauding acts as war crimes. Para 504, U. S. Dep't of Army, Field Manual 27-10, Law of Land Warfare (1956) (Hereinafter cited as FM 27-10) lists non-grave breach war crimes, including: use of forbidden arms or ammunition, abuse of or firing on the flag of truce, use of civilian clothing by troops to conceal their military character during hostilities, maltreatment of dead bodies, violation of surrender terms, and killing without trial of spies or other persons who have committed hostile acts.

II.

STANDARDS OF PROCEDURAL DUE PROCESS UNDER INTERNATIONAL LAW

A. Civil Criminal Laws

Although customary international law has recognized the proposition for some years that an alien, prosecuted before regular criminal courts, should not be denied justice[5], there had been minuscule concentrated effort prior to 1945 to bring to fruition the enumeration of the definitive elements of this concept, save the statement that the alien was entitled to essentially the same treatment as the nationals of the prosecuting state. The moving forces to bring about an explicit meaning of the terms "fair trial"/ denial of justice were the United Nations Human Rights Commission,[6]

---

5.   Wise, Note on International Standards of Criminal Law, appearing in Mueller and Wise, INTERNATIONAL CRIMINAL LAW 135 (1965). An early effort by the United States to obtain damages for denial of justice to one of its citizens is the subject of a comment in 22 Am. J. Int'l. L. J. 667 (1928) and concerns the trial of B E Chattin by Mexican authorities. The Arbitration Commission in that case distinguished between indirect and direct responsibility of states as giving rise to denial of justice and held that liability attaches only when there is "outrage, bad faith, willful neglect of duty or manifestly insufficient governmental action" at p 674. See also Roy, Is the Law of Responsibility of States for Injuries to Aliens a part of International Law?, 55 Am J Int'l L J 863 (1961), for a discussion of the meaning of the term "justice", which he considers to be the "closest possible approximation of that ideal of absolute justice."p 865.

6.   Malik, Human Rights in the United Nations, 6 Int'l J 275 (1951). There have even been considerations of an International Court of Human Rights, together with regional and specialized courts on this subject, Note, 60 Am. J. Int'l. L. J. 68 (1966) The Declaration of Human Rights (19 State Dept Bull. 751) is regarded by US Supreme Court as a pledge by this country to the international community, Oyama v California, 332 U.S. 632 (1948); see Hudson, Charter Provisions on Human Rights in American Law, 44 Am. J. Int'l. L. J. 543 (1950).

in the field of civil criminal laws, and the International Committee of the Red Cross,[7] in the law of war sphere where concern is directed toward war crimes and enforcement of occupation laws.

The procedural due process/fair trial concept in the civil criminal law field concerns the benefits accorded the alien by the municipal law of the prosecuting state and seeks to ensure equal treatment with the nationals of that state,[8] so long as the international standard of minimum rights is not transgressed through the denial or withholding of certain rights. This minimum standard, according to the Declaration of Human Rights adopted by the United Nations General Assembly in 1948, includes the following rights: everyone has the right to life, liberty, and security; freedom from arbitrary arrest; fair and public trial by an independent and impartial tribunal; and that the presumption of innocence applies until proven guilty.[9] This declaration is regarded by Professor Gardner as a "yardstick for measuring the progress of governments and peoples in the long struggle for freedom and dignity."[10] A

---

7.   The work of the International Committee of the Red Cross (hereinafter referred to as ICRC) is traced from its origin in 1864 to the Geneva Conventions of 12 August 1949 in a book entitled THE GENEVA CONVENTIONS OF 12 AUGUST 1949 (1949). A detail examination of the task in preparing these Conventions appears in The New Geneva Conventions for the Protection of War Victims, by Pictet, 45 AM. J. Int'l. L. J. 462 (1951).

8.   Orfield, What Constitutes Fair Criminal Prosecution under Municipal and International Law, 12 U. Pitt. L. Rev. 351 (1950).

9.   See 19 State Dept. Bull. 751 (1948)

10.   IN PURSUIT OF WORLD ORDER 241 (1964)

former Chairman of the UN Commission on Human Rights, Mr. Charles

Malik of Lebanan, regards the Declaration on Human Rights as a

milestone in human rights on a par with the Magna Carta, the Bill of

Rights, and observed that: "...we must devise adequate international

machinery which will see to it that the rights defined in the

Declaration are in fact observed and that whenever and wherever

they are violated, something must be done about it."[11] Of course,

this declaration concerns many other individual rights, such as

power, respect, well-being, skill, and security to mention but

a few. Little mention is made today of judicial matters, however.[12]

The United Nations Declaration inspired the establishment

in 1950 of the European Convention of Human Rights which, in

addition to other matters, provides for five basic rights as being

a minimum to a fair trial: inform the accused of the nature of the

charges against him; provide adequate time to prepare his defense;

allow the accused to defend himself or have the services of a

---

11.   Malik, supra note 6. So also, Comment, International
Recognition and Protection of Fundamental Human Rights, 1964 Duke L Rev
866, which traces the historical development of the protection of
human rights, starting with the treaty of Berlin in 1878 which
required recognition of religious freedom. For a review of
problems in Asia and efforts to conform to the UN Declaration, see
Note, International Protection of Human Rights in the Criminal Law:
An Asian Experience, 3 Harv. Int'l. L. Club Bull. 80 (1961)

12.   McDougal and Bebr, Human Rights - Status Today, 58 Am J Int'l
L J 603 (1964), review the concern of human rights in such areas
as power, wealth, well-being, skill, and security; only mentions fair
trial right in passing. For US position on such treaties, see
Harris, UN Adopts International Conventions on Human Rights, 56
State Dept Bull. 104 (1966); critical comments contained in article
by Mr. Korey entitled Human Rights Treaties: Why is the U. S.
Stalling? 45 Foreign Affairs 414 (1967).

qualified attorney to assist him; allow examination of witnesses; and the use of an interpreter.[13] The Convention also provides that a public trial be conducted within a reasonable period of time after the commission of the offense.

Under status of forces agreements entered into by the United States with its NATO allies,[14] Japan and Korea, these countries have agreed to accord the following procedural rights to an accused in a criminal trial: prompt and speedy trial; to be informed, in advance of trial, of the specific charge or charges made against him; to be confronted with witnesses against him; to have compulsory process for obtaining witnesses in his favor, if they are within the jurisdiction of the receiving states; to have legal representation under the conditions prevailing for the time being in the receiving states; if he considers it necessary, to have the services of a competent interpreter; and to communicate with a representative of the Government of the sending State and, when the courts permit, to have such a representative present at his trial. In addition to these rights, the Protocal Minutes with Japan in 1953 included the additional provisions: not to be arrested or detained without being at once informed of the charge against him; to have counsel present; not to be detained without adequate cause and the right to appear in

---

13. Harris, <u>European Convention on Human Rights</u>, Crim. L. Rev. 205 (Apr. & May, 1966). See also, under same title, Note in The Cambridge L. J. (Apr. 1966) concerning the acceptance by the United Kingdom of the right of individuals to petition to the European Commission of Human Rights for a three year period. p. 4-7.

14. 4 U. S. T. & O. I. A. 1792, 1802 (1953)

open court with counsel to contest his detention; public trial by an impartial tribunal; not compelled to testify against himself; full opportunity to examine all witnesses; and no cruel punishments to be imposed.[15]

Assessing the practical effect of the NATO Status of Forces Agreement, LTC Ellert feels that this agreement is working so well in providing a fair trial guide that its provisions should be added to the list of rights for aliens under future international agreements negotiated by the United States, in order that US Nationals would receive such benefits if tried in foreign civilian courts.[16]

Trial before a United States civil court entitles the accused, irrespective of his nationality, to the benefits of the Constitutional safeguards, such as right to counsel, trial by jury, prohibition against ex post facto laws, right against unreasonable searches and seizures, privilege against self-incrimination, to a speedy trial, to be informed of the accusation, to have compulsory process and to confront witnesses, but also the interpretations of the Constitu-

---

15.   4 U.S.T. & O.I.A. 1846 (1953)

16.   Ellert, NATO "Fair Trial" Safeguards, as reviewed by professor Levie, 58 Am.J.Int's.L.J. 823 (1964). Re, The NATO SOFA Agreement and International Law, 50 NW. L. Rev. 349 (1955), discussed the practice of stationing troops in foreign lands and the principle of supremacy of the territorial soverign to try all crimes. In the only case to reach the Supreme Court under the post-World War II agreements of this nature, it adhered to the principle that the territorial soverign had exclusive jurisdiction to punish offenses against its laws committed within its borders, unless expressly or impliedly waived and refused to grant relief where the United States had allowed Japan to try the petitioner. Wilson v Girard, 354 U.S. 524 (1957).

tion by the US Supreme Court which provide additional safeguards
to the individual accused of crimes.[17]

B. Law of War

1. Customary International Law

The law of war is designed to limit the exercise of destruc-
tive power inflicted by one belligerent upon another, to reduce to
a minimum the suffering of war, and to facilitate a prompt return
to peace.[18] The first codification of the rules governing
hostilities was undertaken by Dr. Francis Leiber at the behest of
President Lincoln during the War Between the States and appeared
as General Order Number 100, dated 24 April 1863.[19] The rules
contained therein have been carried forward through the various
international efforts to ensure that wars were carried along the
lines which produced the least suffering by participants and non-
participants alike. Violations of these rules of war resulted in
the imposition of criminal sanctions as evidenced at the end of

---

17.   For example, Abel v United States, 362 U. S. 217 (1960), holding that the Fourth and Fifth Amendment protections against
unreasonable searches and privilege against self-incrimination
extended to the alien accused of conspiracy to commit espionage in
the United States.

18.   Lauterpacht, The Problem of the Revision of the Laws of War,
29 Brit. Yb. Int'l. L. 360, 364 (1952): Lauterpacht, The Limits of
the Operations of the Law of War, 30 Brit. Yb. Int'l. L. 206 (1953).
Q. Wright considers that international law has fallen short in its
efforts to maintain world peace because it has failed to link its
substantive rules with enforcement and correcting procedures, A
STUDY OF WAR 203 (1964).

19.   For an account of the Lieber Code, see Garner, General Order
100 Revisited, 27 Mil. L. Rev. 1 (1965).

World War I in the Leipzig Trials and again at the end of the Second World War. Political considerations militated against war crimes trials arising from the Korean War.[20]

International law requires that the accused not be denied justice when placed on trial for violating the laws of war.[21] In order to determine what is meant by this requirement, it is necessary to look first at the painstaking work by the United Nations War Crimes Commission[22] which was established in 1942 to collect all cases involving the prosecution of war crimes by the Allied forces. This commission not only studied the rights accorded by the Allies to the accused in general but also analysed those trials by the Allies against enemy soldiers, jurists, and others charged with denying justice to nationals of the Allied countries, military and civilians, in order to determine what was considered to constitute denial of a fair trial for which criminal sanctions

---

20.   Stone, LEGAL CONTROLS OF INTERNATIONAL CONFLICTS 357-363 (1954). The United Nations Command prepared a report entitled Interim Historical Report - Korean War Crimes Division (1953) in which thirty-four referrable cases are discussed as being ready for trial, p. 26.

21.   Q. Wright, Due Process and International Law, 40 Am. J. Int'l. L. 399, 402-3 (1946), quotes with approval from the 1922 Draft Convention on Responsibility of States in defining denial of justice:"Denial of justice exists when there is a denial, unwarranted delay or obstruction of access to courts, gross deficiency in the administration of jusicial or remedial process, failure to provide those guarantees which are generally considered indispensible to the proper administration of justice, or a manifestly unjust judgement."

22.   Schwelb, The Works of the War Crimes Commission, 23 Brit. Yb. Int'l. L. 363 (1946).

were applicable. It concluded that the following elements consisted of a fair trial:[23]

    a) fair and impartial tribunal,
    b) accused to know of the charges against him and the evidence against him,
    c) services of a defense counsel and interpreter;
    d) full opportunity to present his defense, including the right to call witnesses and produce evidence before the tribunal; and
    e) in the event of conviction, imposition of a sentence which does not outrage the sentiments of humanity.

2. The 1949 Geneva Conventions

The 1949 Geneva Conventions[24] made two important contributions in the area of war crimes, namely:

    a) established four distinct standards regarding what rights should constitute a fair trial, the application of the

---

23.   These elements are based on review of the twelve cases reported in 5 and 6 LAW REPORTS OF TRIALS OF WAR CRIMINALS (1949) (hereinafter cited as LAW REPORTS), involving prosecutions by the US, British, Australian, and Norwegian courts against accusers, prosecutors, appointing authorities, reviewing authorities, and executioners for denying these rights to the accused military and civilian persons. However, the rule of prejudicial error appears in 14 LAW REPORTS 84 (1949), to the effect that the court must take into consideration not only the error but its consequences.

24.   Geneva Convention for the Amelioration of the Condition of the Wounded and Sick in Armed Forces in the Field, (1955) 6 U.S.T. & O.I.A. 3115, T.I.A.S. No. 3362 (hereinafter referred to as GSW): Geneva Convention for the Amelioration of the Condition of Wounded Sick and Shipwrecked Members of Armed Forces at Sea (1955), 6 U.S.T. & O.I.A. 3217, T.I.A.S. No 3363 (Hereinafter referred to as GWS at Sea); Geneva Convention Relative to the Treatment of Prisoners of War (1955), 6 U.S.T. & O.I.A.S. 3316, T.I.A.S. No 3364 (hereinafter referred to as either the Prisoner Convention or GPW); and the Geneva Convention Relative to the Protection of Civilian Persons in Time of War, 6 U.S.T. & O.I.A. 3516, T.I.A.S. No. 3365 (1955) (hereinafter referred to as the Civilian Convention or GC) (all four conventions came into forces as to the United States on 2 Feb. 1956).

various standards depending on the status of the accused, the nature of the territory when the offense was committed, and the nature of the armed conflict (national or international), and

b) created as a grave breach the wilfully deprivating of the rights of a fair and regular trial to prisoners of war, protected persons, and certain other victims of war, as prescribed by the Conventions.[25]

These four standards and the type of tribunals involved in war crimes trials are reflected on the Diagram at Appendix A and summarized as follows:

a) Article 99 - 108, GPW - enumerated rights for the protection of the prisoner of war who is assimilated into the penal code applicable to the armed forces of the Detaining Power,

b) Article 3, GC - all the judicial safeguards which are recognized as indispensable to civilized peoples is the standard applicable to the unlawful belligerent falling into the hands of the Detaining Power on non-occupied territory during hostilities,

c) Article 64 - 76, GC - enumerated procedural rights to be accorded the unlawful belligerent for trial of war crimes committed during occupation, and

d) Article 146, GC - prosecution of a grave breach entitles the accused to procedural rights which are to be not less favorable than some rights enjoyed by PW's, plus what other safeguards he enjoyed under "b" or "c" above.

---

25.   Art. 50, GWS; Art 51, GSW at Sea; Art 130, GPW; and Art. 147, GC.

Because the prisoner of war is subject to the provisions of the Uniform Code of Military Justice,[26] there is but slight concern in determining the standard of procedural rights he will enjoy in the event of trial by the United States. However, at the other end of the spectrum of certainty as to what elements must be accorded the alien enemy to constitute a fair trial is the standard set forth under Article 3 of the Civilian Convention. (See Appendix B) To resolve the morass question of exactly what procedure will be accorded at all under the 1949 Geneva Conventions, we are confronted with much the same situation as faced Mr. Justice Holmes who lamented because of the lack of procedural rules: "Legal obligations that exist but cannot be enforced are ghosts that are seen in the law but are elusive to the grasp."[27]

The task of this paper is two-fold: to summarize the rules of customary international law regarding a fair trial (the Article 3 standard) and then to examine the effect that the 1949 Geneva Conventions have had upon the customary law. In order to render a proper interpretation of the printed words of these four international agreements, the purposes in causing their creation must be kept always in mind: to benefit the victims of war, not the states. In setting forth a standard of interpretation for the Genocide

---

26. Art. 2(9), Uniform Code of Military Justice, 10 USC §802 (hereinafter cited as either the Code or UCMJ).

27. The Western Maid, 257 U.S. 419, 433 (1922). Wright, Supra note 21 at 406 also points out that the "standards of international law defining denial of justice are unfortunately vague".

Convention, the International Court of Justice stated: "The high ideals which inspired the Convention provide, by virtue of the common will of the parties, the foundation and measure of all its provisions."[28] Thus, our concern is <u>when</u> do the Conventions apply, to <u>whom</u> are they applicable, and <u>what</u> benefits can be claimed under the judicial provisions.

3. Application of the Conventions

Common to the four Conventions is Article 2 which provides that the provisions of the Conventions will apply to all cases of declared war, any other armed conflict of an international character, and in all cases of total or partial occupation.[29] Article 3 of

---

28. Advisory Opinion on Reservations to the Convention on the Prevention and Punishment of the Crime of Genocide, (1951) I.C.J. 15, 23. Pictet states that most international conventions are for the benefit of and primarily concerned with affairs of government; however, these four Conventions are concerned with the principle of respect for human personality. THE GENEVA CONVENTIONS OF 12 AUGUST 1949, COMMENTARY IV, GENEVA CONVENTION RELATIVE TO THE PROTECTION OF CIVILIAN PERSONS IN TIME OF WAR 26 (pictet ed. 1958) (hereinafter cited as COMMENTARY IV).

29. On 11 June 1965, the ICRC took the position that the United States, South Viet-Nam and its allies, and the Democratic Republic of Viet Nam (North Viet Nam) and the National Liberation Front (the Viet Cong) were bound by the terms of the 1949 Geneva Conventions. The United States replied that we would abide by the terms of the Conventions. 60 Am. J. Int'l. L. J. 92-3 (1966) The North Vietnamese government has taken the position however, that the Convention does not apply to trial of prisoners of war because of a reservation it made (27 U.N.T.S. 340 (1957) denying benefits of the GPW to prisoners of war who are tried and convicted of war crimes. The fallacy of this reservation is examined in Comment, The Geneva Convention and the Treatment of Prisoners of War in Vietnam, 80 Harv. L. R. 851 (1967). The historic development of the organizations operating in South Viet Nam and controlled by Hanoi is covered in Carver, The Faceless Viet Cong, 44 Foreign Affairs 347 (1966).

each Convention is directed solely to armed conflicts not of an international character and brings into application certain minimum benefits to the victims of war which has been described as a "miniture" Convention.[30] In Viet-Nam today, the assistance rendered by the United States and five other nations[31] brings into application the judicial provisions of the Prisoner Convention because the conflict is of an international character. However, because the United States and the other nations allied with South Viet-Nam do not occupy any territory, the judicial provisions contained in Articles 64-67 of the Civilian Convention do not apply to the trial of those who, not being entitled to prisoner of war status, nevertheless engage in the hostilities and are made amen/ able to trial when they violate the law of war. Only Article 3 of the Geneva Civilian Convention is applicable to judicial proceedings by the U. S. against the unlawful belligerent in that situation.[32]

In dealing with the non-PW - the unlawful belligerent -, an

---

30.   Esgain & Solf, The 1949 Geneva Conventions Relative to the Treatment of Prisoners of War: Its Principles, Innovations and Deficiencies, 41 N. C. L. Rev. 537, (1963). Commentary IV 34.

31.   Korea, Australia, New Zealand, the Philipines, and Thailand. 55 State Dept. Bull. 455 (1966).

32.   Pictet, supra note 7 at 473 points out that the Civilian Convention was "an imperative necessity" because of the bitter experiences of World War II and was really aimed at belligerent occupation. However, Article 3 was included as a "fall back" since the states would not agree on any more strong language as originally suggested which would have made the entire Civililian Convention applicable in the event of civil war, colonial conflict or religious wars. COMMENTARY IV 30.

important question exists as to whether he is entitled, in the event of trial for violating the law of war, to the Article 3 or the Article 64-76 standard of due process. The answer turns on whether the territory is occupied and his status. In discussing the application of the Civilian Convention to Occupied Territory, the American Delegate Plenipotiary and a member of the American delegation, Mr. Yingling and Mr. Gunnane, respectively, stated:

"While the Civilian Convention contains no definition of 'occupation', probably nothing more could be added to the principle in Hague Article 42 that "Territory is considered occupied when it is actually placed under the authority of the hostile army." The Convention will not apply in liberated territory of an allied country such as France in 1944 in relation to the United States and the United Kingdom."[33] Thus, in Viet-Nam, the provisions of due process contained in Articles 64-76 do not apply to the trial of an unlawful belligerent because the territory is not occupied territory as intended by the drafters of the Civilian Convention.

Mr. Pictet speaks of the accused's trial in both situations as follows:[34]

> The right of detained persons to a fair and regular trial will be ensured in occupied territory, applying the provisions

---

33.   The Geneva Conventions of 1949, 46 Am. J. Int'l. L. J. 393, 417 (1952).

34.   COMMENTARY IV 58. Article 3, GC was designed to apply to armed conflict which had all the markings of an international conflict, except that the fighting took place within the territory of a single state. COMMENTARY IV 36.

of articles 64-76; there is no special provisions applying to the territory of the Parties to the conflict, but the rule contained in Article 3 will be applicable: i.e., the Court must afford "all the judicial guarantees recognized as indispensable by civilized peoples."

The open-end approach to the Article 3 standard is ameliorated to some extent where the accused is a "protected person" and is charged with committing a grave breach, in which case he is entitled to some of the procedural benefits granted to the PW, which in turn, is dependent on the procedural rights accorded members of the armed forces of the Detaining Power.

4. Persons Entitled to the Geneva Conventions

Thus far we have discussed generally _when_ and _what_ standards are provided by the Geneva Conventions so far as procedural due process is concerned. But _Who_ is entitled to claim the provisions of the Conventions incident to a war crimes trial?

The Prisoner Convention extends to all prisoners of war, these being the members of the armed forces, militia members, and, among others, resistence movements complying with the four-tier requirement to be discussed below. (See Appendix C for definition contained in GPW.)

The Civilian Convention refers to a group of victims of war as "protected persons" who are defined in Article 4 as being:

> Persons protected by the Convention are those who, at a given moment and in any manner whatsoever, find themselves, in case of conflict or occupation, in the hands of a Party to the conflict or Occupying Power of which they are not nationals.
> Nationals of a State which is not bound by the Convention are not protected by it. Nationals of a neutral State who find themselves in the territory of a belligerent

State, and nationals of a co-belligerent State, shall not be regarded as protected persons while the State of which they are nationals has normal diplomatic representation in the State in who hands they are.

In general, the Civilian Convention includes within its ambit two main groups: any one who is not a national of (1) the Party to the conflict or (2) Occupying Power into whose hands he falls.[35]

For example, the Civilian Convention would not apply in the event of a national of the U. S. were to fall into the hands of the U. S. in Viet- Nam. Similarily, a national of a neutral State, or one not bound by the Conventions, would not be entitled to the protected person status should he fall into the hands of any of the five co-belligerents in Viet-Nam.

5. Grave Breaches

In addition to the question of whether the Conventions apply and, if so, what portions, is the matter of grave breaches, a type of international war crime. Common to the four Conventions are the following criminal acts included within the grave breach definition: willfull killing, torture or inhumane treatment, including biological experiments and wilfully causing great suffering or serious injury to body or health, willfully depriving a person entitled to the Convention in question of the rights of fair and regular trial prescribed in the particular Convention, and

---

35.   COMMENTARY IV 45059.

extensive destruction and appropriation of property not justified by military necessity and carried out unlawfully and wantonly.[36] The GPW adds to this list the crimes of compelling a prisoner of war to serve in the armed forces of the hostile Power. The unlawful deportation or transfer or unlawful confinement of a protected person is added by the GC, which also includes within the grave breach definition compelling a protected person to serve in the armed forces of a hostile power, the taking of hostages. Grave breaches defined in the GSW and GSW at Sea add additional crimes acts not here relevent.

The four Conventions place upon the Contracting Parties these three obligations regarding grave breaches:[37]

a) to enact any national legislation necessary to provide effective penal sanctions for those having complicity as to a grave breach;

b) to search for such persons charged with complicity as to a grave breach; and

c) to try such persons before its own courts, or to hand over for trial to another High Contracting Party where a prima facie case is established.

---

36.   Art. 50, GSW; Art. 51, GSW at Sea; Art 130, GPW; and Art. 147, GC.

37.   Art. 49, GSW; Art.50, GSW at Sea; Art. 129, GPW; and Art. 146, GC. These articles have been described as the "cornerstone of the system used for the repression of breaches of the Convention." COMMENTARY IV 590. Before the US Senate Committee conducting hearings on the Geneva Conventions, the Assistant Attorney General stated:

The four Conventions also places upon the Parties the duty to repress all other violations of the provisions of the Conventions as well as other crimes and states that those entitled to benefit from the Conventions shall be entitled to the safeguards of a proper trial and defense.

"We have laws that cover all those subjects." (emphasis added) Hearings Before the Committee on Foreign Relations, US Senate, 84th Congress, 1st. Sess., 3 June 1955, on the Geneva Conventions for the Protection of War Victims 28. As later discussion will reveal, the United States has very few laws to effect the purpose of these treaty obligations. The drafters of the Conventions considered it would be necessary to enact some additional legislation, THE GENEVA CONVENTION OF 12 AUGUST 1949, COMMENTARY III, GENEVA CONVENTION RELATIVE TO THE TREATMENT OF PRISONERS OF WAR 629 (Pictet ed. 1960)(hereinafter cited as COMMENTARY IIIO. For a review of the need for federal criminal legislation since there is no federal common law on crimes, see Bilder, Control of Criminal Activity in Antartica, 52 Va. L. Rev. 231, 246-7, 269-279 (1966) for an example that the need for US lagislation in overseas areas is not limited to the topic of law of war, but also affects vitally treaty commitments in other areas of our foreign relations.

III.

JURISDICTION TO TRY WAR CRIMINALS

A. Basic Principles

At the threshold of any discussion of criminal law lies
the topic of jurisdiction - the authority or power of the State
to act in regard to the trial and punishment of a person charged
with violating the law, in this case the law of war. Customary
international law recognizes five basic principles of jurisdiction,
all of which are applicable to the general topic of war crimes:
territorial, nationality, passive nationality, protective,
and universality.[38]

The territorial principle is perhaps the most widely
applied and accepted one. It provides that the State may exercise
its jurisdiction as to prescribing laws regarding all crimes
committed within its borders and to enforce such laws, with certain
exceptions not here pertinent. This power to act as to all matters
within its territory is one of the most important attributes of
sovereignty.[39] The second and third category listed above are
concerned with nationality: if the offender is national of State X,
the active personality (or nationality) principle applies to give

38.   Carnigie, Jurisdiction Over Violations of the Laws and
Customs of War, 39 Brit. Yb. Int'l. L. 402 (1963).

39.   Beckett, The Exercise of Criminal Jurisdiction over
Foreigners, 6 Brit. Yb. Int'l. L. 44 (1925) outlines the development
of the modern state on a territorial basis.

that State jurisdiction over his conduct; where the victim of the criminal conduct is a national of State X, that State can make ameniable to its criminal powers the offender when and if he comes into the custody of State X, under the passive nationality principle. Speaking of the passive personality principle, Judge Moore of the Permanent Court of International Justice stated:[40]

> It appears to be now universally admitted that when a crime is committed in the territorial jurisdiction of one state as the direct result of the act of a person at the time corporeally present in another state, international law, by reason of the principle of constructive presence of the offender at the place where his act took effect, does not forbid the prosecution of the offender by the former state, should he come within its territorial jurisdiction.

The fourth category, protective principle of jurisdiction, allows a State to exercise its criminal laws where the offense involved is harmful to the vital interests of the state, as in the instance of mass deportation of populations.[41]

The fifth principle, universality, allows any state to punish any offender for a criminal act, irrespective of the nationality of the victims or where the crime was committed.[42] Traditionally, its application was evidenced in the case of pirates seized

---

40.   The case of the S. S. "Lotus", (France v Turkey), Permanent Court of International Justice, Ser. A, No. 9. (1927); 2 Hudson World Court Reports 20 (1935)

41.   Note, Protective Principle of Jurisdiction Applied to Uphold Statute Intended to have Extra-territorial Effect, 62 Colum. L. Rev. 371 (1962), discusses United States v Luteak, 344 U. S. 604 (1953) the War Brides Case.

42.   Carnigie, Supra note 38 at 405.

on the high seas where there was technically a legal vacuum. This principle holds that there must be some law for the repression of unlawful conduct and thus serves as a gap-filler. The trials of war criminals after World War II utilized this principle for the exercise of jurisdiction by the military and civilian courts where, for example, an Australian military commission tried a Japanese charged with committing offenses in Java against Chinese and Indians, and also a United States trial in Germany of a German accused of crimes against Czechoslavak and Russian nationals which were committed at a time before the United States even entered the war against the Axis.[43]

Professor Cowles, in his article entitled "Universality of Jurisdiction over War Criminals", sets forth the rule which was followed by most all of the Allied war crimes tribunals:[44]

> Actual practice shows that the jurisdiction assumed by military courts, trying offenses against the law of war, has been personal or universal, not territorial. The jurisdiction, exercised over war criminals, has often been of the same nature as that exercised in the case of pirates, and thus broad jurisdiction has been assumed for the same fundamental reasons. *** But, while the State whose nationals were directly affected has a primary interest, all civilized States have a very real interest in the punishment of war crimes.

As early as 1919, the international community generally recognized that individuals as well as States could be held crimi-

---

43.   United States v Remmele, 15 LAW REPORTS 44 (1949)(discussed but not reported). This fifteen volume represents the work of the UN War Crimes Commission and will be referred to herein after as LAW REPORTS.

44.   33 Cal. L. Rev. 176. 217 (1945).

ally liable for the commission of war crimes.[45] However, it remained for the events of World War II to bring forth the exercise of any full scale criminal jurisdiction in the field of international criminal responsibility.[46] Unfortunately, the Restatement of International Law prepared by the American Law Institute failed to recognize the application of the universality principle to war criminals,[47] and was content to adopt the outmoded approach which was valid until 1919 that this principle applied only to pirates, thus disregarding the approval of the UN General Assembly in 1948 of the

---

45.   Customary international law was once an obstacle to the advancement of human rights because this doctrine provided for only states as subjects of international law, but it is now being eroded. E. Lauterpacht, Some Concepts of Human Rights, 11 How. L. J. 264 (1965). The establishment of universality of jurisdiction for the trial of war criminals is regarded as an expansion of customary international law in the direction of the greater protection of human rights, Brand, The War Crimes Trials and the Law of War, 26 Brit. Yb. Int'l. L. 414 (1949). See also Q. Wright, War Criminals, 39 Am. J. Unt'l. L. J. 257, 262 (1945). The Council of the Conference of Paris of 1919 recognized the right of the Allies to punish individuals for violations of the laws of war; see 14 Am. J. Int'l. L. 117 (1920) for discussion of this Conference.

46.   In the context of law of war, Q. Wright, supra note 45 at 284-5, refers to the four systems of law and their advantages: national law - precise rules and procedure, but apply in the United States, and are not designed to vindicate international law; law of war - also has established rules and procedure, but is not suited for the development of the law of peace; law of peace - establishment of an international tribunal to discourage future law breakers; and universal law - ideal system.

47.   Section 35, Universality; for critical evaluation of the Restatement's provision dealing with jurisdiction, see Metzger, The Restatement of the Foreign Relations Law of the United States: Bases and Conflicts of Jurisdiction, 41 N.Y.U. L. Rev. 7 (1966).

Nuremberg Judgment.

The principle of universality of criminal jurisdiction was used by the United States military commissions and military government courts after the Second World War throughout the world.[48] Often times, the consent of the injured State was obtained prior to the United States commencement of a proceeding for crimes committed outside the US zone of Germany.[49] The judgment of the International Military Tribunal which tried major war criminals in Nuremberg stated that its jurisdiction came from the Charter promulgated by the Allied Powers and on the basis of a territoriality claim in the sense that the four Allied nations stood in the shoes of the defeated

---

48.   LAW REPORTS 23-48 (1949) reviews the jurisdictional basis of the Allied trials of war crimes. See also Section V, C, _infra_. In 1960, Eichmann was kidnapped in Buenos Aires and taken to Israel where he was tried the following year on fifteen counts of crimes against the Jewish people under a 1950 statute of the Israeli government /The Nazi and Nazi Collaborators (Punishment) Law/57107 , war crimes, and membership in hostile organizations. He was sentenced to death and the sentence was executed in 1962 after the Supreme Court of Israel rejected his appeal and the President of Israel denied clemency. The Court exercised jurisdiction under the universality principle because the accusd's conduct must be regarded as international criminal acts and on the basis that every nation has a duty to prosecute those accused of such crimes. The appellate court based its decision the 1907 Hague Regulations, the _Lotus_ case, and the Judgment of the International Military Tribunal at Nuremberg which was adopted by the United Nations General Assembly. In reviewing this case, Mr. Fawcett approves of the exercise of jurisdiction and observed: "There is evidence then that the majority of states have accepted the principle that there are certain crimes _jure gentium_ for which any state may assert jurisdiction to try and punish the offender. On this principle there would be concurrent jurisdiction between States and the exercise of that jurisdiction would fall to the _forum conceniens_.", The Eichmann Case, 38 Brit. Yb. Int'l. L. 181, 207 (1962).

49.   For example, the United States obtained permission from Belgium to try offenses committed against Belgium nationals in Belgium, see the Malmedy case, (United States v Bersin et al) discussed in Koessler, _American War Crimes Trials in Europe_, 39 Geo. L. J. 18, 38 (1950).

sovereign resulting from the deballatio of Germany. The trial of the major war criminals in Tokyo, however, based its jurisdiction on the formal instrument of surrender in which Japan consented, by the express terms of the document, to such trials.[50]

B. The 1949 Geneva Conventions

The Prisoner and Civilian Conventions both expressly recognize the right of the Detaining or Occupying Power to subject prisoners of war, protected persons, and others to the laws of that Power and international law in force at the time of the commission of the conduct in question.[51] Specifically, Article 82 of the GPW provides that the prisoner of war is subject to the laws, regulations, and order in force in the armed forces of the Detaining Power. Article 64 of the GC allows the Occupying Power to subject the population to those measures which will maintain an orderly government and insure the security of the Occupying Power, and Article 5 envisions trials by the Detaining Power of those charged with espionage, sabotage and other hostile acts, committed during the conflict or occupation.

---

50.   Carnigie, supra note 38 at 413-6.

51.   Carnigie, supra note 38 at 406, points out that conventional war crimes are partly covered by customary international law and partly by the 1949 Geneva Conventions. The Conventions will govern those states parties thereto and to strangers who agree to its principles, with the greatest impact being on the grave breaches provision regarding jurisdiction. When two or more states ally to repel an aggressor or to wage war, each can exercise jurisdiction as to those captives in its custody without regard to territorial rights of one state; in other words, there is no requirement for waiver of jurisdiction to be obtained from the territorial soveriegn in order to try a person accused of war crimes.

27

IV

CONSIDERATIONS AFFECTING PROSECUTORIAL DISCRETION

A. Staff Judge Advocate Duties and Responsibilities

The Staff Judge Advocate of each command has the responsibility to supervise the conduct of a war crimes program[52] and to assure that proper action is taken at his level of command.[53] In the discharge of these duties, the SJA is available to the commander and the staff to give advice regarding the investigation of a war crimes incident, the status of an accused, conditions of detention, as well as the sufficiency of evidence for the purpose of either prosecution or a request for extradition or transfer of custody of an enemy alien to US control.[54]

In drafting the charges, the relevent facts must be averred so as to place the accused on notice of the conduct in question.

---

52.   Paragraph 3.47g, U. S. Dep't. of Army, Field Manual 101-5, Staff Officers' Field Manual (1964)

53.   Paragraph 40, U. S. Dep't. of Army, Pamphlet 27-5, Staff Judge Advocate Handbook (1965). Although the US Army Reserve provides for War Crimes Teams (TO&E 27-500g) which are under the control of The Judge Advocate General of the Army, there are no such units now in the active Army. Letter of 9 December 1966 from the Chief, International Affairs Division, Office of The Judge Advocate General to the Assistant General Counsel, Department of Defense.

54.   Acting under US Military Assistance Command, Vietnam (hereinafter referred to as MAC-V), Directive No. 20-4, dated 25 March 1966, the Staff Judge Advocate is required to conduct a thorough review of all war crimes incidents which are investigated by lower echelons.

Charges against a prisoner of war should be placed upon the same forms used in the trial of members of the US armed forces.[55] There is no particular format in the drafting of the specification and, as the Supreme Court stated in rejecting as assignment of error on the basis of defective charges and specifications: "Obviously, charges of violations of the law of war triable before a military tribunal need not be stated with the precision of a common law indictment."[56] Also, there is no set of rules (such as in the case of court-martial trials) as to the elements of the offense of the various war crimes, but an excellent treatment of grave breach violations of the Prisoner Convention is given by Professor Howard S. Levie,[57] and the UN War Crimes Commission has dealt with the elements of other war crimes.[58] In addition to the criminal conduct involved, the specification should allege the nationality of the accused and the victim, the position held by the accused, and that the conduct "was in violation of the law and custom of war." Admitting that there is no single source in deciding whether

---

55.   Paragraph 12, Appendix 6c, Manual for Courts-Martial, 1951, 471 (hereinafter cited as MCM, 1951.)

56.   In re Yamashita, 327 U. S. 1, 17 (1946).

57.   Penal Sanctions for Maltreatment of Prisoners of War, 56 Am. J. Int'l. L. 433, 444-454 (1962); Professor Levie of Saint Louis University School of Law was formerly chief, International Affairs Division, Office of the Judge Advocate General.

58.   15 LAW REPORTS 89-154 (1949). Also see Greenspan, THE MODERN LAW OF LAND WARFARE 463-502 (1959).

a given offense constituted a war crime, Chief Judge Quinn of the US Court of Military Appeals stated:[59]

> The test bringing these offenses within the common law of war has been their almost universal acceptance as crimes by the nations of the world. This test is consistent with the rule, already noted, that the common law of war has its source in the principle, customs, and usages of civilized nations.

B. Custody of the Accused

Of primary concern to the Staff Judge Advocate, once authorization for the conduct of war crimes trials is granted, is not only the sufficiency of the evidence to support the conclusion that there is a referrable case but also whether the command has custody of the persons responsible for the violation of the law of war. If the US has custody, there is little concern regarding his presence in court. However, the absent accused raises many collateral problems once his whereabouts is known: can he be extradited from the country of asylum to the country where the US is providing military assistance, can he be merely returned to US control once he is found in a foreign country, and what is the situation where he flees to the United States to avoid prosecution for crimes committed in the zone of operations.[60]

Extradition to or from the United States territorial

---

59. <u>United States v Schultz</u>, 4 C.M.R. 104, 114 (1952).

60. Lauterpacht, <u>Law of Nations and Punishment of War Crimes</u>, 21 Brit. Yb. Int'l. L. 58, 86 (1944).

jurisdiction is governed by over eighty bi-lateral treaties, the 1933 Montevideo Convention,[61] and by Section 3181 of Title 18 of the United States Code which provides that extradition will take place only during the existence of a treaty of extradition with a foreign government involved. However, since the state of war has been regarded as suspending the application of extradition treaties,[62] the argument that the United States, or other nations, can merely request surrender of fugitives in time of war from countries where the fugitives are found to be located has merit. This argument has added merit when the country of asylum is a High Contracting Power to the Geneva Conventions and the offense is a grave breach.[63] Even when the United States has an extradition treaty, such a treaty might not apply to crimes committed outside the US jurisdiction in any event because most treaties allow for the extradition only when the crime took place within the territorial jurisdiction of the United States, such jurisdiction being defined to include territory under the control of or belonging to one of

---

61.   Note, The New Extradition Treaties of the United States, 59 Am. J. Int'l. L. J. 351 (1965) considers the three treaties entered into since World War II involving Brazil, Sweden and Israel.

62.   Mr. Justice Stewart, when a member of the 6th Circuit, considered the effect of war on an extradition treaty between the United States and Italy and held that the 1945 peace treaty provided for the revival of all former bi-lateral treaties between the countries which had been suspended when the U. S. declared war on Italy in 1941. Argento v Horn, 241 F. 2d 258 (6th Cir. 1957)

63. COMMENTARY IV 52-58.

the contracting states.[64] Perhaps the best approach would be for the government of South Viet-Nam to request the extradition and then release custody to the United States upon the return of the fugitive to South Viet-Nam. This course of action would be feasible where the surrendering state did not require the requesting state (South Viet-Nam) to prosecute, otherwise, the US could transfer the file to South Viet-Nam for prosecution.

Where the fugitive flees to a country other than the US, he might be returned to US control for purposes of trial in South Viet-Nam without the formality of an extradition process. Such was the case after World War II when the Allies agreed to surrender requested persons held in custody to another Allied Power.[65]

In the event the fugitive seeks asylum in the United States or its territories, he might be subject to extradition under a

---

64.   Note, _supra_ note 61 at 354.

65.   The Moscow Declaration of 1943 requested the Allies to surrender war criminals to the demanding state, Morgenstern, _Asylum for War Criminals,_ 30 Brit. Yb. Int'l. L. 382 (1953). The establishment and operation of civilian internment enclosures and prisoner of war camps in Germany following the WW II is discussed by General Telford Taylor, Chief of Counsel for the Subsequent Proceedings held at Nuremberg, in FINAL REPORT TO THE SECRETARY OF THE ARMY 50-58 (1949)(hereinafter referred to as Final Report), who observed that expeditious handling of cases was of prime concern in view of the instability of the country and the large number of persons sought for trials as accused and often times as witnesses in other trials by different countries. The Allies in WW II recognized their failure to include in the Treaty of Versailles in 1919 a provision for the surrender of war criminals, thus the provision in the Moscow declaration, 39 Am. J. Int'l. L. J. 565 (1945) The Austrian Government has requested that Brazil extradite recently arrested Franz Stangl to stand trial for war crimes arising from his activities while commandant of Nazi concentration camps at Treblinka and Sobibir in Poland during WW II, _New York Times,_ 4 March 1967, p. 3, col. 7.

treaty but he is not subject to extradition under Section 3185 of
the above US Code Title, because this statute, enacted in ~~the~~ 1900
in order to return to Cuba from New York a US citizen wanted by
the US military Governor of Cuba for postal crimes,[66] is applicable
only where the US has complete or exclusive control of the foreign
country, such as in the case of occupation.[67] Political offenses
are excluded from extradition treaties as a general rule.[68] Efforts

---

66. Ln _Neely v Henkel_, 180 U. S. 109 (1900), the Supreme Court
held that there was no constitutional prohibition to enactment of
extradition law (18 USC §3185) for retroactive effect since the law _merely_
changed procedure and did not create a new criminal offense, thus
not offending the principle of ex post facto. Also, the Court held
that the petitioner, seeking to bar his extradition to Cuba which
was then under the control of the US Army, had no constitutional
rights to a certain kind of trial by the demanding state or territory.
H Report No. 1625, 56th Congress, 1st Sess. 2(1900). Such a statute
as proposed in 1954 or an extradition treaty with South Viet Nam
would be necessary to fill to present vacuum existing due to the
lack of such a treaty and legislation. (_Treaties in Forces as of_ 1
January 1966 fails to list such a treaty between the United States
and Viet Nam, p 210-211. (State Dep't. Publication No. 8042).

67.   _In re Krausman_, 130 F. Supp. 926 (DC Conn, 1950), held
that the United States must have exclusive jurisdiction over the
territory in order to seek return of petitioner (former employee
of American Express Co. in Berlin) and that the relinquishment of
jurisdiction to Germany during proceedings mooted the extradition
proceeding under 18 USC § 3185.

68.   Garcia-Mora, _Crimes Against Humanity and the Principles of_
Non-Extradition of the Political Offenders, 62 Mich. L. Rev. 927
(1964); see _Artukovic v Boyle_, 140 F. Supp. 245 (SD Cal, 1956) where
extradition request under Treaty with Serbia in 1902 was denied by
the US court where the murders charged by Yugslovia (regarded as
the proper successor to the Treaty) were regarded as political acts.

in the House of Representatives in 1954 to liberalize this statute

failed. It was proposed then (a) to allow for extradition from

the United States to a foreign country occupied exclusively or

jointly by the US and (b) to increase the list of crimes for which

extradition was possible to include many occupation types offenses.[69]

No further action has been taken by the Executive to suggest the enactment

of the legislation providing for extradition to countries from the

United States where the US is engaged in collective security

measures.[70]

---

69.   For review of the House action, see Note by Fairman in 48
Am. J. Int'l. L. J. 616 (1954).

70.   The US courts have stead-fastly held by the words of Chief
Justice Marshall: "Our Constitution declares a treaty to be the law
of the land. It is, consequently, to be regarded in Courts of
Justice as equivalent to an act of the legislature, whenever it
operates of itself without the aid of any legislative provisions.
But when the terms of the stipulations imports a contract, when
either of the parties engages to perform a particular act, the
treaty addresses itself to the political, not the judicial department;
and the legislature must execute the contract before it can become
a rule for the Court," in Foster v Baker, 2 Peters 253, 314 (1829)
(noted in 44 Am. J. Int'l. L. 545) as being the foundation for the
principle of self-executing and non-self-executing treaties. The
precise terms of the Conventions require legislative action by the
Congress, but the Assistant Attorney General's position is repeated:
"We have laws that cover all those subjects" when referring to the
Geneva Convention requirements to enact legislation, see Hearings,
supra note 37.
        Addition comments on extradition: (1) Neutrals are extremely
reluctant to allow for the extradition of war criminals and have the
right under international law to grant or refuse asylum as it sees
fit, unless bound to act otherwise. Neumann, Neutral States and
Extradition of War Criminals, 45 Am. J. Int'l. L. 495 (1951). The
US Supreme Court considers this principle of international law in
Factor v Laubenheimer, 290 U. S. 276 (1933), giving liberal construction to an extradition treaty with Britain.
        (2) Irregular extradition methods, such as kidnapping, have
never been the grounds for the court to state there had been a denial
of justice. Evans, Acquisition of Custody over the International

C. Determination of Status

1. The Prisoner of War

The traditional division between the armed forces and the peaceful population, and between lawful and unlawful belligerent has been preserved by the Geneva Conventions. These Conventions divide the persons falling into the hands of a Party to the conflict into two groups primarily: Prisoner of war, and "Protected persons". Under Article 4 of the GPW,(see Appendix C), eight categories of prisoners of war are listed and include members of the armed forces of a Party to the conflict, militia making up part of the armed forces, and members of other militia or volunteer corps (resistence movements) who comply with the following four tier formula:

a) carry arms openly

b) have a fixed distinctive sign,

c) be commanded by a person responsible for that unit, and

d) conduct operations in accordance with the law of war.

PW status is also accorded those who suddenly take up arms upon the approach of the enemy (levee en mass), persons who

_____

Fugitive Offender, 40 Brit. Yb. Int'l. L. 77 (1964), considers the claims of denial of justice raised by Soblen (199 F. Supp. 11 (1961), Eichmann, Argoud (kidnapped in Munich in 1963 and tried in France as leader of military revolt against President DeGaulle), and Ahlers (editor of Der Spiegel) who fled to Spain, deported to Germany for treason trial, but conviction set aside by Federal Supreme Court of Germany on other grounds in 1965. See also O'Higgins, Unlawful Seizure and Irregular Extradition, 36 Brit. Yb. Int'l. L. 279 (1960), for review of British cases. The US Supreme Court has also ruled that kidnapping of accused in order to secure his presence in court does not impair the power of the court. Kerr v Illinois, 119 U. S.

accompany the armed forces (civilian members of aircraft crews, war correspondents, supply contractors and the like), merchant marine crews, and those members of the armed forces in a neutral country who are interned there.

The main concern here is to determine whether there has been compliance with the four tier formula in the case of militia or volunteer corps. Because so many times, the enemy combatant in Viet-Nam fails to comply with this formula which has existed since the Hague Regulations of 1907, there is a considerable task in determining the status of captives falling into the hands of the US armed forces in Viet-Nam. The key to entitlement to PW status has boiled down to the wearing of a distinct uniform, one that readily sets the wearer apart from the civilian population.[71]

2. US Practice in Viet-Nam

The United States has established tribunals under Article

---

436 (1886)(seized in Lima, Peru and brought to Chicago for larceny trial) and Frisbie v Collins, 342 U.S. 519 (1952)(Michigan officials seized wanted murderer in Chicago held not to violate due process; "...sound basis of due process of law is satisfied when one present in court is convicted of a crime after having been fairly apprised of the charges against him and after a fair trial in accordance with constitutional procedural safeguards", in opinion of Justice Black, at p. 524.)

71.   Baxter, So-Called 'Unprivileged Belligerency': Spies, Guerrallas, and Saboteurs, 28 Brit. Yb. Int'l. L. 323, 342 (1951). Paragraph 74, FM 27-10, provides that persons otherwise entitled to PW status (members of armed forces etc.) lose their right to PW treatment whenever they deliberately conceal their status for military advantage. An excellent historical development of treatment accorded prisoners of war is contained in Kooks, PRISONERS OF WAR (1924), especially p. 7, 34, and 370.

5 of the GPW for the purpose of determining the status of those captives about whom there is doubt as to status.[72] The applicable regulation[73] provides for a 3 member tribunal to be convened by the general court-martial authority and that at least one member of the tribunal be a judge advocate officer. The proceeding before the tribunal is informal and a summarized record is prepared. The detainee is entitled to the following rights: counsel (either a judge advocate officer appointed by the general court-martial convening authority or a fellow detainee; an interpreter; to present his case and call witnesses; and be present with counsel in open sessions of the tribunal. Evidence of a relevant nature is admissible, the technical rules of evidence being dispensed with in order to establish the truth of the issues involved. The tribunal is granted the power to call witnesses, obtain documentary evidence and real evidence, as well as the power to determine the mental and physical capacity of the detainee. Decisions are reached by a majority vote on all issues; in the event of a tie vote on the ultimate issue of whether he is entitled to PW status, the decision is in favor of granting PW status.

---

72. Article 5, GPW provides: "Should any doubt arise as to whether persons, having committed a belligerent act and having fallen into the hands of the enemy, belong to any of the categories enumerated in Article 4, such persons shall enjoy the protection of the present Convention until such time as their status has been determined by a competent tribunal."

73. MAC-V Directive No. 20-4, dated 25 March 1966.

When PW status is granted, a brief resume is prepared by the tribunal. In the event PW status is not granted, a summary of the evidence and pertinent documents are forwarded to the convening authority and then to the SJA, MAC-V for review. The MAC-V SJA has the authority to order a rehearing or may grant PW status without further action. Detainees who are determined to be civil defendants by the US (this group includes terrorists, spies, saboteurs, or criminals) are turned over to the proper South Vietnamese authorities for possible trial and punishment under the laws of that country.[74]

The present policy of the United States is not to exercise its right to try any prisoners of war against whom there might be sufficient evidence to establish a violation of the law of war and to transfer all PW's to the control of the South Viet-Nam Army as provided in Article 12, GPW. The civil defendants are also turned over to the local authorities, even though the United States may have been the victim of a violation of the law of war.[75] The US is

---

74. In an article entitled "The United States Achievements in Viet Nam", General Wheeler, Chairman of the Joint Chiefs of Staff, reported that the US had captured 6,000 enemy on the battlefields in 1965 and 9,000 during 1966. 56 State Dept. Bull. 186, 191(1967). A news release by the MAC-V Headquarters in Saigon (reported by the New York Times, 25 January 1967, p 1, col. 1) indicates that the US has 2,500 PW's, about half considered to be members of the North Vietnamese Army and the rest Viet Cong. See Westerman, International Law Protects PW's, Army Digest 32-39 (February 1967).

75. In such cases, the accused are subject to trial by a military court where a majority vote controls all issues, evidence of probative value is admitted, and the accused is represented by counsel who is entitled to know the nature of the charges and to present evidence on behalf of the accused. Westerman, Military

hopeful of repatriation of PW's and has released several Viet Cong prisoners (with approval of the South Viet-Nam government) in expectation of reciprocal action on their part.[76]

3. The Unlawful Belligerent

The Prisoner Convention was designed to provide a definition of prisoner of war broad enough to include all lawful combatants in land warfare within the protection afforded by international law. It is a matter of record that there are individuals taking part in the conduct of hostilities in Viet-Nam who do not qualify as prisoners of war. The Civilian Convention, being an innovation and a supplement to Hague Regulations Number IV of 1907, tried to protect in specified ways the inhabitants of occupied territory and in a general way others who fell into the hands of a Party to the conflict. As was mentioned earlier, the four standards of procedural due process set forth by the two Conventions depend to a great extent upon the status of the accused and the nature of the

Justice in the Republic of Viet Nam, 31 Mil. L. Rev. 137 (1966). In one such trial, the self-confessed Viet Cong agent who killed a member of the South Vietnamese Constitutient Assembly was sentenced to death by a military court in January 1967. New York Times, 11 January 1967, p 3, col. 5.

76.   Article appearing in Washington, D. C. Post, 29 January 1967, p. 1, col 3. The Detaining Power may, if it desires, grant asylum to PW's who do not wish to be repatriated. Baxter, Asylum to Prisoners of War, 30 Brit. Yb. Int'l. L. 481 (1953). Paragraph 197, FM 27-10, states that belligerents may exchange prisoners of war, but are under no duty to do so.

territory.[77]

The failure to specify certain procedural safeguards for
the guerrilla fighter conducting operations in the home territory to
one of the Parties to an armed conflict of an international character
has an impact upon detention problems, judicial proceedings, and
other areas because the Conventions were designed to apply primarily
to a fixed area of land being occupied by a hostile armed force.[78]
However, the modern guerrilla fighter: the unlawful belligerent: was
not forgotten by the drafters of the Civilian Convention, as indicated

---

77.   COMMENTARY III 52-61, outlines the inclusion of partisans
in the definition of prisoner of war in order to give to these proper
belligerents, whether acting in their own country or elsewhere,
would be given proper treatment in the event they fell into the hands
of the enemy. But, to benefit from the Prisoner Convention, such
personnel must qualify under the four-tier formula, otherwise they
are regarded as unlawful belligerents. The US Dep't. of Army Field
Manual 31-21, Special Forces Operations (June 1965) paragraph 12d,
dealing with resistence movements, overt and covert, points out
that PW treatment is accorded to only those wearing the uniform
(as to regular army personnel) or complying with the four-tier formula
(as to indiginous personnel operating against the enemy.)

78.   Pictet, The New Geneva Conventions for the Protection of
War Victims, 45 Am. J. Int'l. L. 462, 473-5 (1951) reports that
the Civilian Convention was really aimed at the conduct of the
belligerent occupant. The type of warefare now in Viet Nam is
a legal novelty of sorts because there has not been such international
armed action of extended duration of this nature. Tilman, The Non-
lessons of The Malayan Emergency, Military Review 62 (December 1966).
Background material for the interested reader regarding resistance
warefare in France, Yugoslavia, Malaya, Algeria, Greece, the
Philippines, and Palestine, is covered in UNDERGROUNDS IN INSURGENT,
REVOLUTIONARY AND RESISTANCE WARFARE (1963), a publication of the
Special Operations Research Office, American University.

in the following remark:[79]

> It may, nevertheless, seem rather surprising that a
> humanitarian Convention should tend to protect spies,
> saboteurs, or irregular combatants. Those who take part
> in the struggle while not belonging to the armed forces
> are acting deliberately outside the laws of warfare. Surely,
> they know the dangers to which they are exposing themselves.
> It might have been simpler to exclude them from the
> benefits of the Convention, if such a course had been
> possible, but the terms espionage, terrorism, banditry
> and intelligence with the enemy, have so often been used
> lightly, and applied to such trivial cases, that it is not
> advisable to leave the accused at the mercy of those
> detaining them.

Mr. Pictet was speaking of Article 5 of the GC which allows

for the partial derogation of the Convention where the security

of the Detaining Power is threatened by hostile acts during occupation

or otherwise. The Protecting Power will continue to function, how-

ever, in such an event.[80] The irregular or unlawful belligerent

is therefore covered by the GC as a "protected person" and entitled

to trial under the standard of due process, dependent upon where

he was captured during occupation or fell into the hands of the

Detaining Power as a result of the conflict.[81] The unlawful

---

79.   COMMENTARY IV 53. See also Nurick and Barrett, Legality
of Guerrilla Forces Under the Laws of War, 40 Am. J. Int'l, L. 563 (1946).

80.   Common to the four Conventions is the Article (Art 8, GSW,
GSW at Sea, and GC and Art 9, GPW) providing for the appointment by
the belligerents of a Protecting Power to ensure compliance with
the Conventions - a most onerous task, says M. Mictet in his
Commentary on the GPW at p 88. The belligerents are under a duty
to appoint such agents. Should the Detaining Power be unable to
secure a suitable Protecting Power, it is then under a duty to obtain
the assistance of a neutral nation, or the ICRC to perform the duties.
(Art 10 of GSW, GSW at Sea and GC, and Art 11, GPW). For an account
of the need for supervision, see TREATMENT OF BRITISH PRISONERS OF
WAR IN KOREA 31-32(1955), as reviewed in 49 Am. J. Int'l. L. 431
(1955).

81.   Supra note 34.

belligerent is not punished _per se_ for being an unlawful belligerent, but rather because of his violation of the law of war on the basis of his conduct, such as murder, sabotage, espionage.[82]

Professor Cowles traces the origin of today's unlawful belligerent to the ancient practice of brindage, under which bands of fugitives from the law would follow along behind the armies, looting and pillaging in the wake of the hostilities.[83] In 1863, Dr. Leiber described this activity as involving armed prowlers and placed them in the same category as pirates. The pirate and the brigand both hope to obtain impunity for their crimes where there is no well organized police or judicial system at the place where their operations are conducted.

A body of international and national law grew up around the activities of the brigand. In the United States, Congress authorized in 1864 the punishment of those guerrilla maurauders because of their failure to operate in accordance with the law of war.[84] In 1926, Roumania presented the problem of controlling the brigand to the Committee of Experts of the League of Nations which concluded that brindage and piracy were to be placed in the same category in

---

82.   Baxter, _supra_ note 71 at 342.

83.   _Universality of Jurisdiction Over War Criminals_, 33 Calif. L. Rev. 176. He defines the term 'brigand' as coming from the word 'briguer', meaning to beg, and classifies Sparticus as a prime example of a freebooter and one of many of this kind who headed independent states in view of their control of the land, at p 183.

84.   13 Stat. 356.

regards to jurisdiction and punishment. In 1924, the Geneva

Convention placed prohibitions on the robbing and ill-treatment of

the wounded and dead by both civilians and members of the armed

forces who fell into this ~~despicable~~ despicable practice, a most unfortunate

by-product of war. Upon capture, of course, they then, as now,

claimed to be legitimate combatants, entitled to PW status.

Today, an unlawful belligerent is punished in view of the

danger he presents to the opponent.[85] This differential of treatment

is based upon the principle of 'legitimacy of combatancy' because

international law does not permit every person to engage in the

hostilities; otherwise, the horrors of war would be indeed

aggravated. Dean Hingurani of the University of Gorakhpur, India,

in his doctorial thesis for Yale Law School, noted:[86]

---

85.   In reply to the ICRC's request that the United States abide
by the Geneva Conventions, the US Secretary of State indicated that
the US would do so but also pointed out: "As you are aware, those
involved in aggression against the Republic of Viet Nam rely heavily
on disguise and disregard generally accepted principles of warfare."
60 Am. J. Int'l.L. J. 92 (1966) The ICRC recognizes this problem by
asking that the life of any combatabt taken prisoner be spared if
he is wearing a uniform or bearing an emblem clearly indicating
his membership in the armed forces.

86.   PRISONER OF WAR 18 (1963). The loss of US citizenship has
been the subject of several cases wherein the government claimed the
US national had lost citizenship by serving in a foreign armed forces
within the meaning of 8 USC § 1481 (a)(3). The principal question
facing the courts was whether such service was voluntary (United
States ex rel Marks v Esperdy, 203 F. Supp 389 (SD NY, 1962) held
service as an officer of La Cabana prison being in charge of the
execution of death sentences imposed by military tribunals, wearing of uniform, and instructing at military school, constituted
service in armed forces of Rebeal Castro Army). Circuit Court reversed
issuance of writ of habeas corpus on other grounds, 315 F. 2nd 673
(2d Cir. 1963) and an equally divided Supreme Court affirmed the
deportation order, 377 U. S. 214 (1963). In 1958, the Supreme Court
reversed decision expatriating a native born US citizen because his
service in the Japanese Army was not shown to be a voluntary act,
Nishikawa v Dulles, 356 U.S. 129.

The right of committing legitimate hostilities is thus restricted to a few categories of belligerent personnel who are so authorized - on the basis of reciprocity - by national and international prescriptions. Such personnel - normally armed forces - are given preferential status of PW's. The rest of the combatants *** are considered to be violators of international law..."

In an excellent article regarding the status of belligerents, Professor Baxter states:[87]

Once it has been discovered that the accused is not entitled to treatment as a prisoner of war, there appears in most circumstances to be no reason in law to inquire whether the individual is a civilian or a disguised soldier for it would appear in the latter case that the soldier, even in occupied territory, is to be regarded as having thrown in his lot with the civilian population and to be subject to the same rights and disabilities."

Although denied PW status and branded as unlawful belligerents, this group is subject to criminal sanctions only in the event they are charged with violations of the law of war, not because of their status alone. To those who feel that patriotism is sufficient justification to entitle the unlawful belligerent to PW status, one must remember that patriotism and humanitarianism work both ways - where one or more patriotic individuals wish to engage in hostilities in order to make for a better tomorrow in their homeland, let them comply with the four tier formula established by the international community so that they would qualify as a PW by letting their status be known.[88]

---

87.   Baxter, supra note 71 at 340.

88.   General Westmoreland, Commander in Chief, MAC-V, estimates that there were 280,000 enemy in South Viet Nam as of the summer of 1966, consisting of the following groups: main-force North Viet Nam Army - 110,000; guerrills or militia - 112,000; political cadre - 40,000; and support units - 20,000. 55 State Dept Bull. 335, 337

D. Other Considerations

1. Duty to Prosecute

Common to all four of the 1949 Conventions is the duty to search out those responsible for responsible for committing grave breaches and either try them before national courts or turn them over to a State requesting to try them and upon a showing of a prima facie case.[89] Parties to the Conventions are also under a duty to supress all other crimes which violate the Conventions, such as pillaging,[90] taking hostages, and failing to protect a PW from insults and public curiosity.[91]

2. Former Jeopardy

The Prisoner Convention specifically prohibits punishment twice for the same act or charge (Article 86) but the Civilian

---

(1966). The fact that the enemy "sometimes lack uniforms" is pointed out in U.S. Dep't. of Army, Pamphlet 360-521, dated 10 June 1966, Handbook.for US Forces in Vietnam. In the Hostages case, infra note 97, the judgment held that the guerrilla is a hero in the eyes of his country but a war criminal as to the enemy which can so treat him upon capture and that there is no other way for the Army to protect itself against such gladfly tactics by those who are not belligerents and thus not PW's. at p 1243.

89.   Art 49, GSW; Art 50, GSW at Sea; Art 129, GPW; and Art 147, GC.

90.   Art 33, GC (Pillaging) and Art 34, GC (Taking hostages).

91.   Art 13, GPW. US fliers have been paraded through the streets of Hanoi, Los Angeles Times, 1 July 1966, p 1, col 3. The Jewish Documentation Center in Vienna, Austria, headed by Simon Wiesenthal, accused the Austrian Government of laxity in the failure to prosecute about 1,000 Austrians for war crimes committed during World War II, New York Times, 3 November 1966, p 5, col 4. Thus, individuals can createpublic opinion regarding the enforcement of the rules of war.

Convention is silent on this point. The United State rule against being placed twice in jeopardy is incorporated into the treatment of war criminals in the case of the PW who is a beneficiary of such a rule contained in the Uniform Code of Military Justice.[92] The international community is more concerned with the imposition of punishment, rather than the matter of jeopardy.[93] Thus, the acquittal, on grounds of duress, of the Mauer brothers by a Salzburg, Austrian court in February 1966 for their part in the mass executions of Jews in Poland was set aside and they were duly convicted in a Vienna court in November of that year and sentenced to eight and fifteen years imprisonment. The jury decision in Salzburg was set aside by the trial judge on the basis that the jury's conclusion as to duress was an 'obvious error' and ordered the retrial.[94]

Depending on the circumstances, there would be no bar to the trial of an unlawful belligerent a second time where no punishment had been imposed resulting from the first trial conducted by either the United States or by an Allied Power who transferred custody of the accused to the US where the first trial is set aside for sufficient reasons and that the second trial will not result in punishment greater than imposed for the first trial.

---

92.   Article 44, UCMJ. The declaration of a mistrial because of military exegencies regarded as not barring a second trial in Wade v Hunter, 336 U.S. 684 (1949).

93.   Snee & Pye, Due Process in Criminal Procedure: A Comparison of Two Systems, 21 Ohio State L. J. 467, 499-501 (1960).

94.   New York Times, 9 November 1966, p 1, col 2.

3. Nullum Crimen Sine Lege & Drafting Charges

Perhaps the greatest single attack mounted against the war crimes trials following the end of the Second World War was that the tribunals were enforcing laws which did not exist at the time of the commission of the alleged criminal act.[95] Examination of this criticism discloses it was directed primarily at the crimes against peace category for which only the major war criminals before the two I.M.T.'s were charged with committing,[96] thus leaving unscathed the many thousand of other proceedings involving crimes against humanity and conventional war crimes. This is not to say that those accused of conventional war crimes and crimes against humanity did not assert that their prosecutions violated the maxim.[97] Some

---

95. See Notes, Symposium: War Crimes Trials, 24 U. of Pitt. L. Rev. 73 (1962) which deplores the unjust nature of the tribunals and regard these trials as being "a ritual of revenge"(p 137); and Snyder, It's Not Law - The War Guilt Trials, 38 Ky. L. J. 81 (1949) which fairly shouts the position taken by this instructor at Brooklyn Law School.

96. For example, see Schwartzenberger, The Judgment at Nuremberg, 21 Tul. L. Rev. 329, 344-351 (1947) and the dissenting opinion of Justice Pal in the I.M.T. for the Far East

97. In the Hostages Case (United States v List et al), infra note 148, one of the twelve Subsequent Proceedings, the tribunal's judgment pointed out that Control Council Law defining the offenses of war crimes, crimes against humanity, and conspiracy, was not defective as being ex post facto in nature because the court found that there was pre-existing international law which had declar ed such conduct to be unlawful. The judgment also pointed out that customary international law did provide a definite standard of proof. XI, Nuremberg Military Tribunal 1240 (1951).

credence was initially found in their claim of retroactive effect because the civil law countries' penchant for legislation brought about the enactment of laws during and after the war which had the effect of declaring illegal conduct committed prior to its enactment. Those countries following the common law had little, if any, trouble in this area because resort for prosecution was based on customary international law and certain treaties, such as the Hague Regulations of 1907 and the 1929 Geneva Prisoner Convention, in order to create substantive offenses and maximum punishments.

The courts of the civil law countries found little difficulty in upholding the convictions on the basis of the tardy legislation, however. In reviewing this matter, Professor L. C. Green finds no prohibition in international law for the enactment of criminal laws having a retroactive effect and states emphatically: "It is not even possible to assert that such legislation is contrary to general principles of law recognized by civilized nations." Judge Musmanno in the _Einsatzgruppen_ case states: "No one can claim with the slightest pretence of reasoning that there is any taint of _ex post factoism_ in the law of murder."[98]

The point is that there is no requirement under international law that there be a law against the conduct charged as violative of the rules of war in order to make out an offense before a United States war crimes tribunal.[99] Turning again to Professor Green who,

---

98.   _The Maxim Nullen Crimen Sine Lege and the Eichmann Trial_, 38 Brit. Yb. Int'l. L. 457, 464 (1962).

99.   Snee & Pye, _supra_ note 93 at 474-478.

in referring to those situations where there was a law with retro-active effect, had this to say: "Moreover, proper analysis of the situation leads to the conclusion not that the law contravenes the maxim nullen crimen sine lege, nulla poena nisi crimen, but that, in providing the machinery for punishing obnoxious crimes, it is an application of the principle ubi crimen ibi poena."[100]

The Prisoner and Civilian Conventions grant the Detaining or Occupying Power the right to exercise jurisdiction for violations of its laws or international law in force at the time the said act was committed. Thus, the Geneva Convention drafters adopted both the common law and the civil law approach to the problem regarding what laws can serve as the basis for prosecution of war crimes.

On this point in the Quirin case, the Supreme Court found that Congress had the power to define and punish offenses against the law of nations under the Constitution and had exercised its authority by sanctioning the jurisdiction of the military commissions to try violators thereof, and that the President had invoked that law by his proclamation establishing the military commission to try the German saboteurs. Mr. Chief Justice Stone went on to say:[102]

---

100.   Supra note 98 at 471.

101.   Art 99, GPW and Art 67, GC contain the principle of charging offenses which existed at the time of their commission, allowing the Detaining or Occupying Power to use its own laws or international law. See discussion, COMMENTARY III 470-1 and COMMENTARY IV 341-2.

102.   Ex Parte Quirin et al, 327 1, 29-30 (1942).

It is no objection that Congress in providing for the trial of such offenses has not itself undertaken to codify that branch of international law or to mark its precise boundaries, or to enumerate or define by statute all the acts which that law condemns. ***Congress had the choice of crystallizing in permanent form and in minute detail every offense against the law of war, or of adopting the system of common law applied by military tribunals so far as it should be recognized and deemed applicable by the courts. It chose the later course.

Approval of this course of action by Congress in adopting the common law of war by reference was continually recognized throughout the judicial review phase of the World War II war crimes involving the Supreme Court and this rule of law is no less valid today whether the tribunal be a general court-martial or a military commission. It is of interest to note that the Congress has sanctioned also the military commission in the Uniform Code of Military Justice, although none of its provisions apply to the military commissions.[103]

An example of the problem facing the civil law countries regarding the retroactive effect of their war crimes laws and an explanation of the method of extrication from the application of the maxim nullum crimen sine lege is found in the 1946 decision by the Supreme Court of Norway in the case of the Director of Public Prosecutions who was charged with torturing and ill-treating civilians during 1944-45. The trial was conducted under the Provisionsl Decree of 4 May 1945 which the accused claimed was invalid because it had retroactive effect. Article 97 of the Constitution of Norway provided that: "No law may be given retroactive effect."

---

103.   Art 21 UCMJ. U.S. Dep't. of Army, Pamphlet 27-174, Military Justice - Jurisdiction of Courts-Martial 13-15 (1965).

Although the Civil Criminal Code provided for the crime charged, the punishment had been increased from imprisonment to death. The Court, in upholding the death sentence, did as the common law countries do: relied upon international law which allowed for the imposition of the death sentence for most all war crimes in general and this crime in particular. Although this case concerned punishment, it serves as an excellent example to demonstrate that international law does not require a written law as to either the substantive offense or the punishment to be in effect at the time of the commission or omission giving rise to a war crime charge.[104]

In drafting charges, the Staff Judge Advocate can rely on the common law of war fountain from which to draw for non-grave breach offenses, but the absence of necessary legislation by Congress renders the fountain virtually bone-dry in the case of grave breach offenses. As pointed out by Professor Levie, other countries, notably the United Kingdom, have enacted laws to execute the grave breach portion of the 1949 Geneva Conventions and suggests that "the United States would be well advised to follow their example.[105]

In the case of the prisoner of war, the UCMJ provides only limited enumerated offenses, such as murder, kidnapping, maltreatment, aggravated assaults, and the general Article (Article 134) allows for the punishment of persons subject to the Code for crimes

---

104.   Decision of each of the thirteen Supreme Court justices and a summary of their views reported in 3 LAW REPORTS 3-11 (1948).

105.   Penal Sanctions for Maltreatment of Prisoners of War, 56 Am. J. Int'l. L. 433, 455 (1962).

and offenses not capital. No such limitations attend the drafting of charges in the case of the unlawful belligerent because the drafter is permitted not only to draw on the common law of war, as is the drafter in the case of the prisoner of war, but, as will be discussed later, can charge the same conduct as capital.

In summary, the Staff Judge Advocate is free to charge as violations of the law of war those offenses derived from the customary international law or the applicable treaties, there being no requirement that the crime charged be set forth in writing prior to the commission of the criminal act.

4. Statute of Limitations

The Uniform Code of Military Justice (Article 43(a) and (d)) provides that a person charged with murder may be prosecuted without regard to limitations of time and that the statute does not run when the accused is outside the jurisdiction of the United States. Where the US Forces are situated in another country to render military assistance, as in Viet-Nam and do not thereby gain any territorial control over the area of operations, the statute of limitations would not run. It would run, however, where the US had exclusive control over the territory, as in the case of belligerent occupation.[106]

---

106. But see Article 43(f), UCMJ, which provides for the suspension of the statute of limitations as to limited crimes: fraud against US, acquisition or disposition of real estate of personal property of the US, or procurement matters.

An additional grant of holding in abeyance the statute of limitations is found in Article 43(e) which provides:

> In the case of an offense the trial of which in time of war is certified to the President by the Secretary or the Department to be detrimental to the prosecution of the war or inimical to the national security, the period of limitations provided in this article shall be extended to six months after the termination of hostilities as proclaimed by the President or by a joint resolution of Congress.

As to the unlawful belligerent who falls into the hands of a Party to the conflict during the conflict or occupation, there is no mention in the Civilian Convention as to a limitations period, although a prompt trial is required once he is in custody of the Detaining or Occupying Power.[107] The international law likewise fails to provide a requirement that an offense be prosecuted within a certain period of time. So, under Article 3 of the Civilian Convention, the unlawful belligerent could be prosecuted before a military commission of the US at any time, but of course trial should be conducted as soon as possible. At the present time, Germany and Austria continue to conduct war crime trials for offenses committed over 20 years ago and there is no objection from

107.   Art 103, GPW requires that judicial proceedings be conducted as quickly as possible, but Pictet indicates that the drafters did not seriously consider that PW's would be tried during hostilities because of inability to secure relevant evidence, COMMENTARY III 626. Art 71, GC requires similar dispatch as to the trial proceedings; see also COMMENTARY IV 354-5. There was no assertion of denial of due process when Hirota was tried before the IM.T. - Far East for crimes against peace committed during his term as Minister of War of Japan from 1933-1938, infra note 133 at 1158-1161.

the international law standpoint, even in those cases where the accused (who often took another name) resided within the prosecuting country.[108]

As a practical matter, the trial of war criminals would take place after the termination of hostilities and before the conclusion of a peace treaty. Additional trials beyond this period would probably be left to the territorial sovereign or another nation under the protective or universality principles of jurisdiction for prosecution and in accordance with the terms of the peace treaty.

5. Record of Trial

Despite the fact that the Code does not require a verbatim copy of a record of trial, the Manual for Courts-Martial, 1951, does impose such a requirement on trials by general courts-martial.[109] The prisoner of war tried by a general court would be entitled to a verbatim copy, even though the Prisoner Convention is silent on the need for a record of trial of any description to be maintained except that the prisoner of war is entitled to the same procedural benefits as members of the armed forces of the Detaining

108.   It is expected that the United Nations Human Rights Commission will accede to a request from West Germany that a proposed convention on the non-applicability of the statute of limitations to war crimes and that the convention delete application of the convention to crimes for which the statute of limitations has already run. In Germany, which has abolished the death punishment, it extended the limitations in 1965 until 1969 for the prosecution of World War II war crimes. New York Times, 7 March 1967, p 2, col 3.

109.   Paragraph 82g.

Power.

The unlawful belligerent, under either the Article 3 or the Articles 64-76 standard of due process, is not entitled as a matter of right to a record of trial, nor is there a requirement that the detaining power maintain one. However, the US should follow the practice of keeping a record of trial in all war crimes trials, and that a verbatim copy be maintained in all cases referred as capital.

The practice followed by the Allies during the World War II trials was to maintain verbatim records of only the I.M.T.'s cases and the Subsequent Proceedings at Nuremberg, all other trials were summarized. No copy was furnished the accused but he and his counsel were permitted to examine it in the prosecutor's office.[110]

6. Interpreters and Translators

The trial of war crimes cases will involve the services of both interpreters and translators, both for the benefit of the accused and the prosecution.[111] An interpreter assigned to assist

---

110.   The original record of the proceedings before the I.M.T. at Nuremberg is now in custody of the International Court of Justice at the Hague, together with the evidence gathered by the commissioners appointed by the Tribunal to gather evidence. There were over 200,000 affidavits filed on behalf of the six organizations accused as being criminal. Harris, TYRANNY ON TRIAL ix (1954). Because of security considerations, the record of trial in the Quirin case was not made available to the public but counsel had access on behalf of their clients. Note, 56 Harv. L. Rev. 631, 642 fn 94. (1943). The record of trial in the I.M.T. - Far East consisted of 48,412 pages, note 133, infra at 133.

111.   Art 105, GPW requires that an interpreter be made available to the accused; COMMENTARY III 487. The Civilian Convention contains

the accused should be regarded as part of the defense counsel's staff and any information he receives must be regarded as privileged information.

7. Transfer of the Accused to an Ally for Trial

Both the Prisoner and Civilian Conventions[112] authorized the Detaining or Occupying Power to transfer captives to another High Contracting Party to the 1949 Geneva Conventions where the receiving Power agrees to follow the provisions of the Conventions and the transferring Power agrees to oversee the treatment, together with the Protecting Power. It is therefore proper to transfer a prisoner of war or an unlawful belligerent to another state for trial of a war crime. In the case of grave breaches, the detaining power is under a duty to either try the accused or release him to the requesting power upon the establishment of a prima facie case. As to non-grave breaches, the Parties to the Conventions are under a duty to suppress all violations of the Conventions, and thus they would be authorized to transfer a captive for purposes of trial, even though the procedural safeguards accorded by the prosecuting

---

the same right of an accused. Art 72 for non-grave breaches and Art 146 requires the accused be given the right to an interpreter. Practice of dual translation into English and German during conduct of Dachau trials, see Koessler, American War Crimes Trials in Europe, 39 Geo. L. J. 18(1950).

112. Ie Art 12, GPW allows transfer and Art 49, GC, forbids only forcibly transfers or deportation of protected persons from occupied territories. There is no prohibition, under Article 3, GC, against the transfer of a captive to another state for trial.

56

Power are considered to be less effective than those of the transferring country.[113] In case a prisoner of war is transfered by the
US for trial before the tribunal of another country, the US might
be subject to pay the expenses of counsel incident to that trial
under the provisions of Section 1037 of Title 18, United States
Code, which was enacted for the primary purpose of providing funds
for the payment of counsel of US personnel before foreign tribunals,
but its wording is broad enough to give rise to such a construction.[114]
In the event of transfer of a prisoner of war, the receiving state
should understand that the US will not pay the expenses of counsel
at his trial and a release obtained where possible, in order to avoid
any doubt as to the applicability of this statutory provision.

---

113.   The US Supreme Court in Neely v Henkel, 180 U. S. 109 (1900),
rejected the claim by the US citizen Neely had a right in a foreign
land to a trial similar to one he would receive in US, saying "But
such citizenship does not give him an impunity to commit crime in
other countries, nor entitle him to demand of right, a trial in other
mode than that allowed to its own people by the country whose laws
he has violated and from whose justice he has fled." at p 123. The
same rationale applies to persons entitled to benefits under the
Conventions. The doctrine of forum conveniens should apply, allowing
the country best suited and has a substantial interest to prosecute
the case.

114.   Although the legislative history reflects the intent of
Congress was to pay such expenses for all personnel serving with,
employed by, or accompanying the Armed Forces, the wording of the
statute and implementing departmental regulation (Section II,
Army Regulation 27-50, 27 May 1966) is broad enough to include the
expenses incurred incident to the transfer of a PW to another
country for trial, even his own country. See U.S. Cong. & Admin.
News p 1731 (1958).

V

WAR CRIMES TRIBUNALS

A. Historical Background

The subject of criminal responsibility for unlawful acts committed during and in furtherance of hostilities reflects a most checkered history. Until the 1700's, the victor was free to exercise summary action over the vanquished, usually in the form of death or enslavement, irrespective of wrong-doing on his part.[115] During the eighteenth century, however, the prevailing practice held that captivity was the best method of handling prisoners, and that death could be meted out only to those captives who had committed serious offenses.[116]

In recent American history is found the trial of Captain Wirz in 1865 for cruel treatment and the killing of Union soldiers held by him at the Confederate Prison at Andersonville, Georgia where he was Commandant. This trial heralded the advent in modern history of the imposition of criminal sanctions upon an individual for conduct in violation of the laws and customs of war. This Confederate officer was tried before a military tribunal and sentenced to death.[117]

---

115.   2 Oppenheim, INTERNATIONAL LAW 367-9 (7th ed, 1952).

116.   2 Oppenheim, INTERNATIONAL LAW 368 (7th ed, 1952).

117.   Levie, supra note 105 at 436.

The application of the principle of criminal responsibility suffered a major set back following the First World War because of the lack of effective plans or programs to insure that those accused of war crimes could be brought before the bar of justice, and because national courts during a period of political instability in Germany were allowed to handle the trials.[118]

This abyss was gapped during the Second World War which experienced a great deal of attention being given to this area. Initially, a United Nations War Crimes Commission was established by the Allies in 1942 to assemble files as to all known violations of the law of war. The Saint James Declaration of 1942, the Moscow and Potsdam Declarations of 1943, and the London Agreement of 1945 reflected the resolute position of the Allied Powers concerning the determination to punish those individuals responsible for crimes of unparalled magnitude in the history of mankind.[119]

This section deals with the framework of the development of the tribunals handling war crimes cases and the impact of the 1949 Geneva Conventions relating to judicial proceedings.

---

118.   Shirer, THE RISE AND FALL OF THE THIRD REICH 58 (1960); Davidson, THE TRIAL OF THE GERMANS 2-3 (1966).

119.   Taylor, The Nuremberg Trials, 55 Colum. L. Rev. 488 (1955) traces the position taken by the United States, starting in 1945, to formulate plans for the prosecution of those who waged aggression and committed other war crimes. The only inclination of a similar position in regards to the conflict in Viet Nam is found in a speach by President Johnson who stated that the second of four essentials for peace in Asia is: "To prove to aggressive nations that the use of force to conquer others is a losing game." 55 State Dep't. Bull. 158, 159 (1966).

B. Types of Tribunals

It is generally accepted that there exists five types of tribunals available for the exercise of criminal jurisdiction over war criminals. These are listed by Professor Glueck as being:[120]

 a. the ordinary domestic courts of the injured state

 b. military or ordinary courts of the accused's state

 c. military commission (common law war court) or other military court

 d. a joint or mixed international military tribunal, and

 e. an international criminal court established for the specific purpose of trying war criminals.

The use of the domestic courts of the injured state for offenses committed within the state is usually an example of the exercise of territorial jurisdiction for the trial of war criminals. The conduct giving rise to the charge of a war crime is most always a violation of the domestic penal law, then the injured state can properly exercise its own jurisdiction in this case, as in South Vietnam at present. Thus, where a recognized government is in existence, the rules of international law dealing with universality of jurisdiction are subordinate to the jurisdiction of the injured state, unless that state is subject to an obligation to do otherwise.[121]

---

120.   Glueck, WAR CRIMINALS, THEIR PROSECUTION AND PUNISHMENT 79 (1944); see also his article, By What Tribunal Shall War Offenders Be Tried?, 56 Harv. L. Rev. 1059 (1942).

121.   Q. Wright, War Criminals, 39 Am. J. Int'l. L. 257, 270 (1945).

By virtue of the 1949 Geneva Conventions, the signatories are required either to try the violator of a grave breach offense or to turn him over to the demanding state. In discharging this obligation, the Parties to the Conventions are bound to use only their own courts, thus discretion is granted by the Conventions as to the forum used, except,where the prosecuting state is an Occupying Power, the Civilian Convention restricts the choice of forums to "its properly constituted, non-political military courts" for the trial of protected persons.[122] The withholding from the regular civilian courts of the exercise of jurisdiction in the event of occupation was based on the ground that such would be regarded as an improper and unwanted extension of the domestic legislation of the occupier, in derogation of the sovereignty of the occupied nations whose laws should be retained in force by the Occupying Power to the fullest extent possible, consistent with its security.[123]

Following the Second World War, many states used their own domestic courts to try war crime cases, as in the case of Norway,[124] Denmark,[125] Poland,[126] and Holland.[127] Few, if any, states conducted

---

122. Article 66, GC.

123.   IIA FINAL RECORD OF THE DIPLOMATIC CONFERENCE OF GENEVA OF 1949 833(1949)(hereinafter cited as II A Final Record).

124.   3 LAW REPORTS, 81 (1947).

125.   15 LAW REPORTS, 31 (1949).

126.   15 LAW REPORTS, 35 (1949).

127.   ibid.

trials of war crimes during the war.

The second category above deals with the use of the courts of the accused's state to prosecute violations of war law against another country. The first time this type court was used proved so unsuitable that serious doubt existed as to resort to such courts in the future. After WW I, the Allies made demand upon the Axis at the Paris Peace Conference for over 800 Germans to be extradited, a demand which was refused because of the unstable political situation confronting the German government. As a compromise, the Allies agreed to permit the Germans to select 45 charged by the Allies with war crimes to be brought to trial. Only twelve were actually tried and of that number half were acquitted and the other six soon escaped from the jails to which they were committed to serve relatively light prison terms for either maltreatment of PWs or, firing on shipwrecked victims.[128] The trial took place before the Criminal Senate of the Imperial Court of Justice in Leipzig in 1921. On the basis of this sad experience the Allies adopted the position early in WW II that the courts of the accused's state should not try any war criminals. However, when the Allied Powers restored control to Germany, that country followed the admirable policy of continuing to prosecute war criminals.[129]

---

128.   Glueck's article, supra note 120 at 1061.

129.   As of 31 March 1961, it is reported that West Germany has tried over 12,700 WW II war criminals in its courts, with 86 receiving the current maximum sentence of life and 5,178 sentenced to a term of years, not to exceed 15 years in prison, Woetsel, THE NUREMBERG TRIALS IN INTERNATIONAL LAW 245 (1962) These trials continue today.

The third category of war tribunals consists of the military courts which were by far the most frequently used forum for the trial of World War II war crimes trials.by the Allied Powers.[130] Acting under the Royal Charter, dated 14 June 1945, the British, Canadian and Australian armed forces established military courts, as did France and Belgium. Luxembourg, by the law of 2 August 1947, established a War Crimes Court composed of both military and civilian personnel. Greece established a Special Court Martial in Athens of mixed civilian and military composition and also provided for the trial of war criminals before a Court Martial of entirely military composition.[131]

Treatment of the United States program of war crime prosecutions by military commission is below.

International tribunals, established by agreement of two or more nations, comprise the fourth category of tribunals. Such were the tribunals which tried the major war criminals in Germany[132] and Japan[133] as well as lesser individuals at the Subsequent Proceedings at Nuremberg[134] and at Yokahama[135], and at Dachau under

---

130.   15 LAW REPORTS, 23-48 (1949).

131.   15 LAW REPORTS, 28-36 (1949). See Dunn, Trial of War Criminals, 19 Australian L.J. 359(1946), for review of the trials conducted under the Royal Charter.

132.   The judgment and sentence of the Tribunal is contained in 41 Am.J.Int'l.L. 172(1949). For views of the Chief Prosecutor of the US, see Jackson, The Trials of War Criminals, 32 ABAJ 319 (1946).

133.   JUDGMENT - INTERNATIONAL MILITARY TRIBUNAL FOR THE FAR EAST (1948)(hereinafter cited as I.M.T. - Far East).

134.   Taylor, FINAL REPORT (1949).

135.   Spurlock, The Yokahama War Trials, 36 ABAJ 381 (1950) and Miller, War Crimes Trials at Yokahama, 15 Brooklyn L. Rev. 191 (1949).

authority of Control Council Law No. 10.[136]

The International Military Tribunal (hereinafter and heretofore referred to as the I.M.T.) at Nuremberg was created by the Allied Powers in the London Agreement of 8 August 1945 for the trial of 24 major Nazis on charges of crimes against peace, war crimes and crimes against humanities, together with a fourth charge of conspiring to commit these substantive offenses. Three individuals were acquitted of all charges and one was tried _in absentia_ (Bormann). Twelve were executed within sixteen days of the sentence being handed down, three sentenced to life imprisonment, and the rest to imprisonment for a term of years. The USSR, France, Great Britain and the United States equally participated in the prosecution of the I.M.T. at Nuremberg.[137]

The I.M.T. for the Far East was established by terms of the Potsdam Declaration and its exercise of jurisdiction was expressly agreed upon by the Japanese government in the Instrument of Surrender of 2 September 1945. All twenty-five accused were convicted on charges similar to the I.M.T. - Nuremberg proceedings and the sentence included seven death penalties, sixteen life imprisonments, and two to a term of years.[138] Judges from eleven nations sat on this

---

136.   Koessler, _supra_ note 111 at 39.

137.   Taylor, _supra_ note 119.

138.   _Supra_ note 133 at 1216-7. The I.M.T. - Far East was established on 19 May 1946 with eleven judges; 35 counts were brought against twenty-eight defendants, two of whom died and one was found unfit to stand trial (p 12); the prosecution presented evidence from June 1946 until January 1947 and the defense from February until January 1948, with the judgment rendered in November 1948.

tribunal.

The Allies exercised jurisdiction in Germany as the occupiers of a conquored nation. A Control Council was established to exercise supreme authority over Germany. On 20 December 1945, the Council promulgated Law Number 10 which provided for the trial of those charged with crimes against peace, war crimes, crimes against humanities, conspiracy to commit these offenses, and membership in certain organizations. These trials were to be conducted by tribunals established within the zone of the respective parties.[139] The concept of a second trial under the London Charter was contemplated but rejected by the Allies in favor of trials under the Council Law No. 10 and within the respective occupation zones of Germany.[140] Upon completion of the I.M.T. - Nuremberg in October 1946, the United States promulgated Ordinance No. 7 for the trial of those charged with the offenses noted above and the twelve cases have been known as the Subsequent Proceedings, conducted from December 1946 until April 1949 (all but two trials had been completed by the Spring of 1948).[141] Before these international tribunals (as later characterized by the US federal courts) came persons from all

139.   Taylor, FINAL REPORT 6-10.

140.   Taylor, supra note 139 at 22-27. Executive Order 9858, dated 21 May 1947, 12 Fed. Reg. 3555; 15 State Dept. Bull. 862 ((1946), pertain to Control Council Law No. 10.

141.   Taylor, supra note 139 at 118-9.

walks of life: diplomats (The Ministers Case[142] and US v Milch[143]),
industrialists (US v Flick,[144] the I G Farben case[145], and US v
Krupp[146]), professional military men (The High Command Case[147] and
the Hostages Case [148]), doctors (The Medical Case[149]), judges,
prosecutors, and other judicial officials (The Justice Case[150]),
and the individuals involved with concentration camps, extermination
units and biological experiments (US v Pohl[151], Einsatzgruppen Case,[152]
and the RuSHA case[153] respectively). Thirty-five of the 148 accused
in these twelve cases were acquitted, twenty-four were sentenced to

---

142.   United States v Weizacker, case 11, reported in vols. VII,
VIII, and IX TRIALS OF WAR CRIMINALS BEFORE THE NUREMBERG MILITARY
TRIBUNALS (1950-51)(hereinafter cited as TRIALS).

143.   United States v Milch, Case No 2, II TRIALS.

144.   United States v Flick, Case No. 5, III TRIALS.

145.   United States v Krauch, Case No. 6, VII and VIII TRIALS.

146.   Case No. 10, IX TRIALS; also reported in 10 LAW REPORTS (1948).

147.   United States v von Leeb, Case No. 12, X and XI TRIALS.

148.   United States v List, Case No. 7, XI TRIALS.

149.   United States v Karl Brandt, Case No. 1, I and II TRIALS.

150.   United States v Joseph Altstotter et al, Case No. 3 III TRIALS.

151.   Case No. 4, V TRIALS.

152.   United States v Ohlendorf, Case No. 9, IV TRIALS.

153.   United States v Greifelt, Case No. 8, IV and V TRIALS.

death and the rest to life or period of years confinement.

Simultaneous with the conduct of the I.M.T. - Nuremberg and Tokyo, individual countries proceeded with the prosecutions, notably the British trial in the fall of 1945 of fourty-five persons for their criminal conduct at the Belsen and Auschwitz concentration camps.[154] The United States conducted a total of around 900 trials involving over three thousand accused persons.[155]

The fifth category of forums available for trial of war criminals is the international criminal court idea which was in vogue for awhile and now has been, in effect, rendered an academic question. Also, aside from the Geneva Conventions, it appears as though participation in this type of court by the United States is barred by the Constitution.

Mr. Kuhn, in his article "International Criminal Responsibility",[156] traces the history of proposals of the creation of such

---

154.   The Belsen Trial (Trial of Josef Kramer and 44 others, as reported in 2 LAW REPORTS (1947); also, the U.S. conducted several trials in 1945, for example the Trial of Josef Hangobl, Case No. 87, reported in 14 LAW REPORTS, On charges of killing unarmed American fliers, and the trial of forty members of the Dachau Concentration Camp staff on charges of cruelties and mistreatment, including killings of many thousands, reported as Case No. 60, 11 LAW REPORTS 5 (1949).

155.   Koessler, supra note 111 at 25 . Aside from the two I.M.T.'s and the Subsequent Proceedings at Nuremberg, the United States Army conducted the following war crimes trials:

Germany	- 491 cases	1,682 accused
Italy	- 9	14
Yokahama	- 297	814
China and		
Philippines	- 108	290

In addition the US Navy conducted twenty trials involving 290 accused at Guam. Interim Report to the US Senate by Senator Homer Ferguson, Foreign Relations Committee, 81st Cong. 1st Sess. 3-4

a court which originated after WWI. The idea was referred to the Commission of Jurists (which body drafted in 1920 the statute for the Permanent Court of International Justice) which recommended its establishment but the League of Nations considered the proposal premature and took no action, despite requests of the International Law Association and the International Association for Penal Law.

After the Second World War, the United Nations also called for a study of the possibility of establishing such a court. At this time (December 1946) the United Nations took action to affirm the principles of the Nuremberg Judgment and called for a codification of those principles. The International Jurists reported back that it was possible to create a criminal chamber to the International Court of Justice, but recommended against the establishment at the time, and made no further effort to codify the laws of war (just as the drafters of the Geneva Conventions avoided any semblence of creating a criminal code.)[157]

Much of the reluctance in the formation of an international

(1949) Apparently, there are no truly accurate figures, for one of US prosecutors at the Yokahama trials reports that there were 952 accused, Spurlock, The Yokahama War Trials, 36 ABAJ 387, 389 (1950).

156.   41 Am. J. Int'l. L. 430 (1947).

157.   Pella, Toward an International Criminal Court, 44 Am. J. Int'l. L. 37(1950), feels that there is a need for such a court; former President, International Association Penal Law. Q. Wright, Proposal for an International Criminal Court, 46 Am. J. Int'l. L. 60 (1952). Report of the International Law Committee, 44 Am. J. Int'l. L. & Doc. Supp. 134 (1950).

criminal court is that the states have traditionally been regarded as the sole subject of international law, and as Professor E. Lauterpacht observed: "... we find that the strangly assorted trio, insurgents, pirates and the Holy See, has been treated as providing the factual basis for denying the absoluteness of the concept of the State as the sole subject of international law."[158] But this doctrinâis being eroded and now individuals may be bound directly to international treaties where the parties (the states making the treaties) so intended.[159] This is the practical effect of the Geneva Conventions regarding criminal responsibility for grave breaches and other violations of the treaties, although the courts of the states were regarded as the proper instrument to carry out the policy, rather than an international tribunal. But there is no rule in international law precluding the creation of an international tribunal by the Convention.

Regarding the question of United States participation in an international court from the constitutional standpoint, Mr. Finch points out that the 1950 draft statute prepared by the International Law Commission for the United Nations[160] would grant to either national courts or the international court such jurisdiction as a treaty might confer upon the courts for the prosecution of war

---

158.   Some Concepts of Human Rights, 11 How. L. J. 364, (1965).

159.   Q. Wright, War Criminals, 39 Am. J. Int'l. L. 257, 262 (1965).

160.   The draft statute provides for: a) application of both national and international law; nine judges, no jury; access gained thru vote of General Assembly of the UN, any organization so authorized by the UN, or a state which has conferred jurisdiction on the Court; indictment to be precise; reasonable time to prepare defense; fair trial facets - right to be present in court, conduct own

crimes under international law.[161]   However, the US Constitution

provides that the Congress has the power to define and punish

crimes against the law of nations[162] and that persons entitled

to the protections of the Constitution (citizens, resident aliens,

and other aliens temporarily within the United States) are

guaranteed <u>inter alia</u> a trial by jury and that such trial must be

held in the state wherein the trial was committed or at such place

designated by Congress when the crime is committed outside any state.[163]

The following constitutional issue is thus framed: does the Congress

or the President possess the authority under the Constitution to

enter into a treaty or other agreement by which a person entitled to

the benefits of the protections of the Constitution is subject to

trial before a tribunal of an international nature, enjoying all of

the safeguards, enumerated in the Constitution but without review

---

defense, qualified counsel, expenses paid, translation of documents,
interpreter, compulsory service to obtian witnesses, and speak on
own behalf; public hearing; majority vote controls all issues;
no appeal; and no subsequent proceedings against same accused on
same charge. 44 Am. J. Int'l. L. Supp. 1 (1952).

161.   Finch, <u>An International Criminal Court: A Case Against
Adoption</u>, 38 ABAJ 644 (1952). Cf The London Agreement establishing
the I.M.T. in Nuremberg and the Genocide Convention of 9 December
1948 which provides for trial of offenders before either national
or international tribunals. The US has not yet ratified this
Convention, or several others in the field of human relations.

162.   U.S. CONST. art. I, § 8, cl 10.

163.   U.S. CONST. art. III, § 2, cl 3.

of the judgment by a federal court.[164]

A partial answer in the negative is found in a closely allied matter which confronted the Nation in 1907 regarding a treaty which would establish an International Prize Court. Because of the constitutional considerations, the Congress entered the treaty subject to a reservation that the United States would be subject to the jurisdiction of this court only in matters of damages for captives declared by the court to be illegal under international law.[165] Ultimately, the International Prize Court befell the same fate as did the proposal for an International Court of Criminal Justice: inaction.

The House of Delegates of the American Bar Association voted against the US entering into a treaty establishing an international criminal court in 1950 and there the matter now rests.[166]

In surveying the distribution of authority in the world since

---

164.   Columbia Law Professor Sager considers that a treaty which would violate the Bill of Rights would be null and void, Charter vs Constitution: An International Criminal Tribunal in American Law, 11 How. L. J. 607 (1965). The effect on the surrender of US nationals for prosecution of grave breaches by a foreign state (either under an extradition treaty or informally) is probably barred where the United States is otherwise in a position to prosecute the accused in one of its courts, except where the US national becomes a part of the enemy force in which case the offender is subject to trial by military commission or even an international tribunal.

165.   Finch, supra note 161 at 647.

166.   38 ABAJ 436 (1950). Q. Wright considers such a court would not be effective in supression of international crimes, supra note 157 at 64-65.

the emergence of the Western state system after the Treaty of Westphalia, Mr. Buehrig notes that the international pattern of authority lacks a capstone and instead of a verticle structuring of authority above the state, we have a lateral expansion of the international community, as manifested by the regional organizations,[167] and the Geneva Conventions which permit the national machinery to handle crimes of an international character.

C. United States War Crimes Tribunals

1. The General Court-Martial

The United States has two tribunals for the trial of war criminals, to-wit: the general court-martial and the military commission. Under the provisions of the Prisoner Convention, authority to prosecute prisoners of war is granted in Article 102 which provides:

> A prisoner of war can be validly sentenced only if the sentence has been pronounced by the same courts according to the same procedure as in the case of members of the armed forces of the Detaining Power, and if, furthermore, the provisions of the present Convention have been observed.

Prisoners of war are made subject to the provisions of the Uniform Code of Military Justice (Article2(9)) and are triable

---

167.   International Pattern of Authority, 17 World Politics 369 (1965). Apparently the United Nations lacks adequate support to step into the Viet Nam situation and remains content to handle smaller conflicts, such as the one in Cyprus, see 56 State Dept. Bull. 179 (1966) for vote on six month extension of the UN PEace Keeping Force there by the Security Council. The UN considers that the present machinery for international criminal sanctions is but an intermediate stage on the way to the true international penal jurisdiction. UN Doc. A/CN. 4/7/ Rev. 1 (1949).

only by general court-martial by Article 18 which reads: "General courts-martial shall also have jurisdiction to try any person who by the law of war is subject to trial by a military tribunal and may adjudge any punishment permitted by the laws of war." Although the Code and implementing Manual for Courts-Martial, 1951, came into existence several years before the US Senate ratified the Conventions, the Conventions were regarded as applicable to the armed forces of the United States[168], however the provisions in the Convention as to sentences were apparently disregarded in Article 18 of the Code, when applied to enlisted prisoners because they would be placed on a par with enlisted personnel of the US and thus subject to the Table of Maximum Punishments, not the law of war. The Table serves as a guide in the case of officers, warrant officers, and others.[169]

Heretofore, all persons charged with "war crimes" by the United States had been tried by a military commission (the common law court which has been properly sanctioned by the Congress and extensively used by the President), irrespective of the status of the accused (except that members of the US armed forces were tried only by courts-martial). Under the terms of the Prisoner Convention and the UCMJ, the United States must try prisoners of war by way of the general court-martial, attended by the same procedure to which US military personnel are entitled.[170]

---

168.   LEGAL AND LEGISLATIVE BASIS, MANUAL FOR COURTS-MARTIAL, 1951-2-4.

169.   Paragraph 127a, MCM, 1951.

170/   For a summary of US prosecutions of WW II PW's for offenses committed during capture and thus tried in general courts-martial, see Manes, Barbed Wire Command: The Legal Nature of the Command Responsibilities of the Senior Prisoner in a Prisoner of War Camp, 10 Mil. L. Rev. 1, 38-40 (1960).

Article 2 of the Code lists those persons subject to the provisions of the Code. Included are prisoners of war in the custody of the United States and excluded are other persons captured during a conflict or occupation. General Yamashita urged that he was entitled to prisoner of war status and therefore should be tried by a court-martial for his pre-capture offenses. But the Supreme Court held that he was not subject to the 1920 Articles of War which were then applicable to trials of US military personnel and that it was proper for him to be tried before a military commission in Manila in 1945 and for depositions and evidence of a hearsay nature to be introduced against him, despite the prohibition of admitting such evidence in the trial of a person before a military commission where that person was otherwise subject to the Articles of War. The Court reasoned that since the accused was not subject to the Articles of War, he could claim none of the benefits provided by the Congress or the President to such persons.[171]

To avoid doubt in the future, the Prisoner Convention now provides:

> Prisoners of war prosecuted under the laws of the Detaining Power for acts committed prior to capture shall retain, even if convicted, the benefits of the present Convention. (Art. 85, GPW) [172]

---

171.   In re Yamashita, 327 U.S. 1 (1946).

172.   This provision is nothing more than the concept followed by most nations in permitting persons convicted under national laws to benefit from such laws. II A FINAL RECORD 570 (1949). In ratifying the GPW, the USSR and other communist bloc nations refused to accept Article 85. Reservations, (1955) 6 U.S.T. & O.I.A. 3467, 3508. Thus, the North Vietnamese government takes a position similar to that taken by the US in the 1940's, but which was to have been cured by Article 85. COMMENTARY III 413-418. For discussion of Hanoi's position, see Comment, The Geneva Convention and the Treatment of Prisoner's of War in Vietnam, 80 Herv. L. Rev. 851, 860 (1967), which concludes that this position is not compatible with the GPW.

The United States' position in the Yamashita case was
that prisoner of war status did not enure to the benefit of one
otherwise so qualifying for PW status where he was charged with pre-
captive offenses, but this is contrary to the US statements
demanding PW status be accorded our personnel charged by the enemy
with war crimes.[173] However it must be recalled that the type trials
conducted against our personnel were pure sham proceedings of the
rankest nature.[174] By way of Article 130, GPW, it is a grave breach
to deny "a prisoner of war of the rights of fair and regular trial
prescribed in the Convention."[175]

As noted earlier, war crimes trials conducted by international
tribunals have been rendered useless for the trial of PWs because
the United States would not permit its armed forces to be tried by
such a tribunal.[176] Also of practical concern is the inability of

---

173.   For example, Case No. 25 in the UN War Crimes reports concern
the US trial of Lieutenant General Shigeru Sawada and three others
charged with the murder of eight Americans following a summary trial,
in derogation of the 1929 Geneva Prisoner Convention. 5 Law Reports
1-24 (1948). An account of the Japanese trial and US reaction is
found in an article by Hyde, Japanese Execution of American Aviators,
37 Am. J. Int'l.L. 480 (1943). (the pilots of the Doolittle Raid on
Tokyo in April 1942).

174.   See cases reported in 5 & 6 Law Reports (1948) and the Justice
Trial, supra note 150.

175.   As noted by Esgain & Solf, even while some of the Allied
courts were conducting trials which did not follow the provisions of
Articles 85 and 102, these same countries were willing to agree that
future such trials would constitute a grave breach of international
law, The 1949 Geneva Convention Relative to the Treatment of Prisoners
of War: Its Principles, Innovations and Deficiencies, 41 N.C.L. Rev. 537,
573 (1963). Pictet reports that German and Japanese troops which fell
into Allied hands after capitulation of these two countries in WW II
were not accorded PW status, COMMENTARY III 74.

176.   Article 17, UCMJ.

a multi-organization, such as NATO or SEATO, to exercise any criminal jurisdiction over captives for the same reason, even where the countries involved (excluding the United States) permitted their military personnel to be tried by an international tribunal. This result is reached on the basis that the Geneva Convention sought to engraph the prisoner of war onto the penal legislation of the Detaining Power and in view of the interesting comments by the ICRC that national law shall not be substituted for international law, the stress being placed on the country capturing the prisoner to try him or else turn him over to a demanding state as provided in Article 147, GPW.[177] Thus, the ad hoc tribunals, such as the I.M.T.'s and those convened under multi-nation agreement for the Subsequent Proceedings, are rendered inappropriate tribunals for the trial of prisoners of war since these tribunals are not within the preview of Articles 85 and 102, GPW, so far as the U.S. is concerned.[178]

2. The Military Commission

a. Historical Development

Kaplan traces this tribunal back to the twelfth century in England when the Court of the Constable and Marshal was established

---

177. The ICRC has opposed the idea that two or more countries can agree to fix responsibility for the care of captives on one country, although the US is doing this properly under the provisions of Art 12, GPW. The ICRC also opposes modification of the GPW to allow an international criminal code to be substituted for national penal laws. Esgain & Solf, supra note 175 at 566-9.

178. Esgain & Solf, supra note 175 at 576.

to determine the rights of prisoners, as well as maintain control over the Army. Gradually, it took over jurisdiction as to all persons and was finally abolished by the Magna Carta in 1215, after which civilians were triable by civil courts. By the time of the American Revolution the British military law had been codified into Articles of War applicable only to members of the military, a practice that the Confederation and Constitution was to follow.[179]

Although the military commission was not legislatively recognized until 1862, military practice recognized such tribunals for the trial of certain persons and offenses incident to hostilities.[180] The trial by the Americans of Major Andre, the British Adjutant General in the US for spying in 1780; of Arbuthnot and Ambrister in Florida in 1818 for inciting the Indians to war against the United States; and of the civilian population during the occupation

---

179. Kaplan, Constitutional Limitations on Trials by Military Commissions, 92 U of Penna. L. Rev. 119 (1943). The first recorded war crimes trials took place in 1305 when a British court convicted Sir William Wallace of violating the laws of war by exterminating non-combatants ("sparing neither age nor sex, monk or man"). The forerunner of the I.M.T. at Nuremberg is traced by professor Schwarzenberger to 1474 when the Allies in the war against Burgundy established a tribunal composed of judges designated by them for the trial of Sir Peter of Hagenbach; The Judgment at Nuremberg, 21 Tul. L. Rev. 329, 330-1, 1947).

180. Quite similar in background, purpose, and legal basis, are the prize courts which are also municipal courts of the United States with authority based in international law. Rowson, Prize Law During the Second World War, 24 Brit. Yb. 160, 162 (1947). The British prosecutor in the Belsen Trial, argued before the military commission that it (the tribunal) was "exactly similar to a Prize Court" and founded on the Law of Nations. 2 Law Reports 70-71 (1948). The military commission was described by Major General Crowder, the Judge Advocate General in 1916 as "our common law war court." S. Rep. No. 130, 64th Cong., 1st Sess, 40.

of Mexico by General Scott in 1847 for specific offenses was being accepted as the proper manner for the maintenance of law and order.[181] These war time tribunals were manifestly needed to fill the legal vacuum created by the normal consequences of hostilities.[182]

The authority for the military commission is found in the common law of war[183] and the Constitution.[184] Under its powers to "define and punish offenses against the laws of Nations", the Congress sanctioned "the creation of such tribunals for the trial of offenses agianst the laws of war..."[185] by enacting Article of War 15.[186] This statutory authority was regarded by the Supreme Court as dispositive of sanctioning the commission. This article provided that "...the provisions of these Articles conferring

---

181.   For an account of the more interesting trials before military commissions, including the accused in the Lincoln assassination plot, Lambdin P. Milligan, and the German Saboteur case, see Kaplan, supra note 179 at 121-2; also the Quirin case, 317 U.S. 1, 31 (1942), for other trials.

182.   Colby, War Crimes, 23 Mich. L. Rev. 482, 487(1925). The commissions have also been described as "simply criminal war courts, resorted to for the reason that the jurisdiction of the courts-martial, creatures as they are of statute, is restricted by law, and can not be extended to include certain classes of offenses which in war would go unpunished in the absence of provisional forum for the trial of the offenders," Howard, DIGEST OF OPINIONS OF THE JUDGE ADVOCATE GENERALS OF THE ARMY (1912)1066-7. But the military commission is more than a provisional forum, as will be developed.

183.   A.W.Green, The Military Commission, 42 Am.J.Int'l.L. 832 (1948). Dr. Lieber, in his work which became General Order No. 100, 24 April 1863 for the guidance of US troops in the field, pointed out in paragraph 13 that military jurisdiction was exercised in two ways: courts-martial (statutory) and military commissions (common law of war).

184.   U.S. Const., art I, § 8, cl 10.

185.   In re Yamashita, 327 U.S. 1, 11 (1946).

186.   AW 15 of the 1920 Articles is the forerunner of today's Article 21 of the UCMJ, both articles having identical wording. The 1920 Articles of War, which were in effect during WW II, were contained in 10 USC § 1471-1593 (1920).

78

jurisdiction upon court-martial shall not be construed as depriving the military commission of concurrent jurisdiction in respect of offenders that by statute or by the law of war may be triable by such military commissions...or other military tribunals."

The Constitution has entrusted to the President as Commander-in-Chief,[187] the power to wage and to carry into effect the laws passed by Congress for the conduct of war.[188] The Congress is granted the power to "raise and support Armies."[189]"to make rules for the government and regulations of the land and naval forces,"[140] and "to make rules concerning captives on land and water."[191] Under its powers to pass laws necessary and proper to effect these enumerated powers,[192] the Congress authorized the President to prescribe such rule of procedure as he deemed proper for courts-martial and military commissions.[193]

In the 1940's the President, in the exercise of these powers and by virtue of his role as sole spokesman for the Nation in

---

187.   U.S. CONST., art. II, § 2, cl 1.

188.   U.S. CONST., art. II, § 2, clauses 1 and 3.

189.   U.S. CONST., art. I, § 8, cl. 12.

190.   U.S.CONST., art. I, § 8, cl. 14.

191.   U.S. CONST., art. I, § 8, cl. 11.

192.   U.S. CONST., art. I, § 8, cl. 18.

193.   For an exhaustive review of the power of the President to issue rules for the conduct of trials by courts-martial, see United States v Smith, 13 U.S.C.M.A. 105, 32 C.M.R. 105 (1962). The congressional grant of such authority for WW II appeared in Article of War 38 and exists today in identical language in Article 36, UCMJ, (10 USC § 836).

regards to foreign relations,[194] authorized the creation of the international tribunals as well as national military tribunals for the prosecution of war criminals. The federal courts were called upon to review his actions and upheld these steps taken in the following particulars: (1) the I.M.T. for the Far East[195] (2) the Subsequent Proceedings at Nuremberg[196]; and (3) the trial by military commission in the United States,[197] in US territories,[198] and in a foreign country,[199] of foreign nationals and US Citizens alike.

After cessation of hostilities, the United States tried cases in Germany by tribunals referred to as Military Government Courts,[200] but they were basically a combination of (a) military commissions in the trial of war crimes and (b) occupied courts in the trial of such matters as curfew violations and carrying fire-

194.   Concurring opinion by Justice Douglas in Hirota v MacArthur, 338 U.S. 197 (1949) and majority opinion in United States v Curtiss-Wright Export Corp., 299 U.S. 304 (1936).

195.   The Hirota case, supra note 194.

196.   United States v Flick, 174 F. 2d 983 (DC Cir, 1949), cert. denied, 338 U.S. 879 (1949).

197.   Ex parte Quirin, 317 U.S. 1 (1942); Note, 56 Harv. L. Rev. 631 (1943); and THE CONSTITUTION OF THE UNITED STATES 450-2(2nd ed 1963).

198.   In re Yamashita, 327 U.S. 1(1946) (the Philippines were then territories of the United States).

199.   Johson v Eisentrager, 339 U.S. 763 (1950)(trial conducted in China and later imprisoned in US facility in Germany when writ of habeas corpus sought.

200.   An extensive review appears in Koessler, American War Crimes Trials in Europe, 39 Geo. L. Rev. 18 (1950) and Fairman, Some New Problems of the Constitution Following the Flag, 1 Stan. L. Rev. 587(1949).

arms.[201] It is unfortunate that the term "military commission" was
not limited only to those cases involving the violations of the law
and custom of war.

The citizenship of the accused before the military commission
is immaterial, the courts holding that it is the nature of the
offense which gives rise to the jurisdiction of the commission without regard to nationality.[202] However, the time, place, and circumstances of the conduct in question is paramount to the determination
of the nature of the substantive offense. It is safe to say that it
is a general rule that an accused, even a citizen of the United States,
has no constitutional right to choose the offense or the tribunal
in which he will be tried. "...It does not derogate from the supremacy
of the civil law or the civil courts to accord to the military
tribunal the full sweep of the jurisdiction vested in it under the
Constitution and the laws thereunder..."[203] At issue in this case
was the objection to the jurisdiction of a military commission to try

201.   An invaluable treatment is given this subject by Nobleman,
American Military Government Courts in Germany, Special Text 41-10-52,
US Army Civil Affairs School (1953), as his doctor‌al thesis.

202.   In the Quirin case, supra note 181, one of the saboteurs
claim‌ to be an American was dismissed by the Court as being of no
importance since the accused had joined forces with the enemies of
his country. The same result in Coplepaugh v Looney, 235 F. 2d 429
(10th Cir. 1956), cert. denied 352 U.S. 1014(1956). Thus, a US
citizen could conceivably join forces with the enemy in Viet Nam
and become subject to trial before a US military commission should
he be charged with violations of the law of war.

203.   Coplepaugh v Looney, supra note 202 at 433. Colonel
Winthrop points out that the military commission's jurisdiction
embraces "enemies in arms." MILITARY LAW AND PRECEDENTS 838 (2nd ed,
1920)(hereinafter referred to as "Winthrop").

a US citizen for espionage in November 1944 and also that he should have been tried in the civilian courts under the charge of treason. Both grounds were dismissed.

b. Its Status Today

Despite the extensive utilization of the military commission twenty years ago in the prosecution of war criminals, it had little congressional recognition at that time and has failed to receive much since then. The traditional war court jurisdiction has been preserved in Article 21 of the Code (as such jurisdiction was preserved by Article 15 of the 1920 Articles of War). The 1951 Manual gives attention to the commission on page 1 by stating that it and the provost courts are proper tribunals for the exercise of jurisdiction under the law of war. The Manual further provides that the military commission will be "guided by the applicable principles of law and rules of procedure and evidence prescribed for courts-martial."[204] In promulgating the Manual, the President thus reserved the authority to himself to change this rule and to prescribe such rules as he deemed appropriate. When President Roosevelt promulgated an Executive Order on 2 July 1942 for the trial of the German saboteurs, he exercised his authority by setting forth the conditions under which the accused would be tried, departing from the rules of evidence prescribed for courts-martial by allowing into evidence matters deemed by the commission to have probative value.[205] This procedure was followed in the

---

204.   Paragraph 2, MCM, 1951. The MCM, 1928 used the same wording.
205.   7 Fed. Reg. 5103 (1942).

82

creation of other US military commissions, all which were authorized
by the President who in turn delegated to the Joint Chiefs of Staff
or other major commands the power to appoint.[206] The same course
of action is open today for the establishment of military commissions.

The military commission is described as:[207]

> A court convened by military authority for the trial
> of persons not usually subject to military law who are
> charged with violations of the laws of war; and in places
> subject to military government or martial law, for the
> trial of such persons when charged with violations of
> proclamations, ordinances, and valid domestic civil and
> criminal law of the territory concerned.

Field Manual 27-10, The Law of Land Warfare, refers to
the military commission as the proper tribunal for the trial of war
crime cases.[208]

The military commission is called into operation only
during times of war and thereafter reverts to a most inactive status.
Despite such paucity of Congressional legislation,[209] it remains an
effective means available to the commander to discharge his

---

206.   For example, see the Coplepaugh case, supra note 202, for
recitation of steps taken to create the tribunal.

207.   U.S. Dep't. of Army REGULATION 320-5, Dictionary of United
States Army terms, changed 2, dated April 1965, at p 247.

208.   Paragraphs 11 and 180, FM 27-10.

209.   Congress has designated The Judge Advocate General of the
Army to receive, revise, and record these proceedings (10 USC § 3037,
and repeated in departmental regulations at paragraph 1c, ARmy
Regulation 1-140); also, the commission is exempted from the judicial
review provision of the Administrative Procedure Act (5 USC § 701 (b)
(1)(F)(1966). Congress has applied the conflicts of interest
enactments to military commissions. 18 USC § 203.

responsibilities in time of war which, surprisingly enough are well described by Chief Justice Stone as follows:[210]

> An important incident to the conduct of war is the adoption of measures by the military commander, not only to repel and defeat the enemy, but to seize and subject to disciplinary measures those enemies who, in their attempt to thwart or impede our military effort, have violated the law of war. The trial and punishment of enemy combatants who have committed violations of the law of war is thus not the only part of the conduct of war operating as a protective measure against such violations, but is an exercise of the authority sanctioned by Congress to administer the system of military justice recognized by the law of war.

The military commission stands on the same quantum of legislative enactments today as it did during the 1940's and remains the duly sanctioned tribunal for the prosecution of war crimes under the Geneva Civilian Convention which also recognizes the right of the Occupying Power to punish protected persons who violate the laws of the Detaining Power before a non-political military court.

D. the 1949 Geneva Conventions

What effect, if any, has resulted from the Geneva Conventions as to the types of tribunals before which war crimes can be prosecuted? Within each of the four standards of due process lies the answer.

The prisoner of war must be tried according to the same courts and according to the same procedures as the members of the armed forces of the Detaining Power. The United States has further provided that the PW is to be tried only by the general court-martial.

---

210.   327 U.S. 1, 20 (1946).

The other three standards of due process, concerning the unlawful belligerent, provide a common requirement: regularly constituted courts. Article 3, GC, provides that the passing of sentences and carrying out of executions must come from a judgment pronounced by a regularly constituted court. Article 66, speaking of trials in occupied lands, requires that the tribunals be "properly constituted, non-political military courts.", when the local courts are not utilized because the offense charged is a violation of the laws promulgated by the Occupying Power or a breach of the law of war. The last standard of due process of law concerns grave breaches. Article 146 mentions a proper trial and defense, with no reference to a tribunal.

Under these four standards, the general court-martial is the proper tribunal for the PW and the military commission, in view of its historical background and Congressional sanction, is the proper tribunal under the three standards specified in the Civilian Convention. The US military government court would be the proper tribunal for non-war crimes committed during occupation.

In regard to international tribunals, all accused, except the PW, would be amenable to trial before such courts under the Civilian Convention which does not prohibit trial by international courts.

An international tribunal can be established by the appointment of the commander having command over the armed forces of two or more nations, such as the United Nations Command during the Korean War. Or, an international tribunal could be created by

following the pattern of the Control Council in Germany, whereby
a central governing agency was established by international agreement
and each of the states represented was free to conduct trials under
their own regulations but based on the authority granted by the
central agency. The situation in Viet-Nam today closely approaches
(if not already surpasses) an international command on the military
level, but for other considerations has not taken on the Korean
War UN Command structure.

VI.

TRIAL OF THE PRISONER OF WAR

A. Procedural Rights Before and During Trial

Many of the procedural rights to be accorded a prisoner
of war on trial for violations of the law of war are well known to
the military practitioner because the prisoner of war enjoys the same
rights as members of the US armed forces. These rights before trial
may be quickly summarized as consisting of: appointment of counsel
at the Article 32 investigation; opportunity to review the charges
preferred against him and to examine the evidence contained in the
prosecution's file; right to call witnesses during the Article 32
investigation; and the services of an interpreter during the entire
judicial proceeding.

The Prisoner Convention sets forth these same rights in
Articles 99 through 108. Care must be given to these provisions
because the validity of the sentence imposed is made contingent
upon three elements: (1) that it is pronounced by the same court and
(2) according to the same procedure in the trial of the armed forces
of the Detaining Power, and (3) that all the provisions of the
Chapter entitled Penal and Disiplinary Sanctions (Articles 82-108)
have been observed.

The first procedural requirement contained in the Prisoner
Convention is to notify as soon as possible both the prisoners of
war in your custody and the Protecting Power of those offenses
punishable by the death sentence.[211] Pre-trial confinement of the

---

211.   Art. 87, GPW.

PW is not permitted per se unless a member of the Detaining Power's armed forces would be confined under like circumstances, or in case of security, but such confinement must not exceed three months.[212] Of course, there is little problem regarding the status of PW and the power to continue custody,[213] the thrust of this requirement goes to the right to a speedy trial (although the conduct of hostilities as well as policy considerations may require a different result).[214] Time spent in pre-trial confinement awaiting trial is to be deducted from any sentence of imprisonment imposed,[215] and the prisoner is not to lose any of the benefits of the GPW, whether convicted or acquitted.[216] There is no prohibition against placing the accused PW in a segregated compound for PW's.[217] Article 12 of the UCMJ forbids placing a member of the US armed forces "in immediate association" with enemy prisoners or other

---

212.   Art. 103, GPW.

213.   The basis for the rule regarding prompt investigation and trial was the experience of WW II. COMMENTARY III 477. Art. 21, GPW allows a belligerent to intern PW's.

214.   The ICRC considered the feasibility of allowing for trials during periods of hostilities because of the disadvantage it may place upon the PW. COMMENTARY III 626.

215.   Art. 103, GPW.

216.   Art. 108, GPW.

217.   See U.S. Dep't. of Army, Field Manual 19-20, Enemy Prisoners of War and Civilian Internees (August 1964), for the administrative handling procedures.

foreign nationals not members of the US armed forces.[218]

Also required by the GPW is a prompt pre-trial investigation. The Convention drafters intended for the accused to have a prompt trial and desired to guarantee this by requiring a prompt "judicial investigation", thus referring to the civil law system procedure for pre-trial investigations. The United States will follow the provisions of the UCMJ, namely Article 32, in the conduct of the pre-trial investigation. During the Article 32 investigation, the accused is entitled to the appointment of a qualified counsel to represent him, as well as the services of an interpreter. The PW must be given a copy of the charge sheet and all allied papers in a language which he understands.[219] Counsel for the accused should also receive a copy of the charges and allied papers. The GPW requires that before trial the Detaining Power advise the PW of the right to the assistance of a fellow prisoner, to the assistance of a qualified attorney of his choice, to call witnesses on his own behalf, and to the services of a competent interpreter. This advice should be reflected by a paper signed by the accused reflecting the above.

The selection of counsel or advocate is initially left entirely with the prisoner. Should he fail to make a selection, the Protecting Power[220] is alloted one week to secure an attorney

---

218.   However, paragraph 18b(2) and paragraph 125, of the MCM, 1951 permits use of the same facilities for both US personnel and PW's.

219.   Art. 105, GPW.

220.   Supra note 80. Neither the North Vietnamese nor the Viet Cong have authorized visits to prisoners they are holding by the ICRC which has requested such authorization. New York Times, 11 October

for the accused from a list furnished by the Detaining Power. The Detaining Power is authorized to appoint counsel where neither the accused PW nor the Protecting Power make a decision.[221] No mention is made in either the Convention or the Commentary by Pictet as to a veto power by the Detaining Power, but security grounds would constitute the sole basis for not allowing counsel to participate where otherwise available to assist the PW. The defense counsel is granted two weeks to prepare for trial and is to enjoy necessary facilities to prepare for the trial; also, he has the right to speak freely with his client, other prisoners of war, and other witnesses, and to the services of an interpreter during the preliminary phase of trial preparation.[222] The interpreter should be assigned as soon as possible, remain throughout the case, and be regarded as a member of the accused's defense for all purposes.

At least three weeks before the trial, the Protecting Power is to be notified of the following data:[224]

> a) name of the prisoner of war, his rank, army, regimental, personal, or serial number, his date of birth, and his profession or trade,

---

1966, p 33, col. 1. The ICRC is allowed by Art. 9 GPW (and by Art. 10 of the other Conventions) to act as a humanatarian organization for the fulfillment of the four Conventions.

221. Art. 35, GPW.

222. Art. 105, GPW.

224. Art. 104, GPW. A copy of the Staff Judge Advocate pre-trial advice, required by Art. 64 of the UCMJ, would satisfy the first three portions of Art. 104, GPW.

b) place of interment or confinement,
c) specification of the charge(s) and applicable legal provisions, and
d) designation of the court which is to try the case, as well as the time and place thereof.

A similar notification is made to the prisoner's representative.[225]

This notification to the Protecting Power and prisoners' representative can best be discharged by forwarding a copy of the pre-trial advice. At the opening of trial there must be a clear showing that the Detaining Power made timely notification to the accused, the Protecting Power, and the prisoners' representative. The Protecting Power is entitled to send trial observers where security permits.[226] In the event that the interests of another state are involved, invitations to attend the proceedings should be extended.[227]

B. Sentencing Powers

The use of the general court-martial for the trial of war crimes offenses charged against a prisoner of war by the United States brings into operation not only the provisions of the Uniform Code of Criminal Justice and Manual for Courts-Martial, but also the Prisoner Convention, all of which place restrictions and prescribe the procedure of the sentencing of these persons found guilty. In general, the applicable penalties are: death, confinement, and forfeitures. Reduction in grade is not permitted, nor is a punitive

---

225. Art. 104, GPW. Art. 79 defines the duties of the PW representative; see also Manes, supra note 170.   x

226. Art. 105, GPW.

227. Such a practice was followed by the Allied countries. Taylor, FINAL REPORT 46 (1949); and The Belsen trial, as reported in 2 LAW REPORTS (1947).

discharge, because these matters are between the PW and his state.

Turning first to the Prisoner Convention it is noted that there is express language allowing the imposition of the death penalty for war crimes and other offenses, but the main thrust of the Convention is toward the procedural aspects, rather than the merits of the penalty or other considerations.[228]

As to punishments in general, Article 87, GPW, provides that prisoners of war are not to be sentenced "...to any penalties except those provided for in respect of members of the armed forces..." of the Detaining Power. In furtherance of this assimilation into the military justice system of law, the prisoners of war who are enlisted are also entitled to the limitations prescribed in the Table of Maximum Punishments, despite the failure of the Manual to so provide.[229]

The court-martial is to be instructed that it must consider "to the widest extent possible, the fact that the accused, not being a national of the Detaining Power, is not bound by any duty of allegiance,..."[230] This requirement thus requires that the court give utmost consideration of the accused's motives in the hopes

---

228.   Art. 101 and Art. 107, GPW.

229.   Paragraph 127a, MCM, 1951.

230.   Art. 87, GPW. This is designed to allow the tribunal to particularize the punishment to the guilt of the accused and to ensure that the tribunal is aware of the PW's lack of allegience to the prosecuting state. Pictet, COMMENTARY III 429-420. A sample instruction to be given by the Law Officer in the trial by a US general court-martial appears as Appendix XXXIV, U.S. Dep't. of Army Pamphlet 27-9. Military Justice Handbook - THE LAW OFFICER (1958).

that the court or reviewing authority will find extenuating circumstances, especially where the accused believed that he should act as he did.[231]

Article 87 provides that the above statement be brought to the attention of the court in order to have a valid sentence imposing the death penalty,[232] although such instruction should be given in all cases. There must be a six month wait from the time the Protecting Party is notified of the imposition ~~of the imposition~~ of the death penalty until its execution.[233] Although there was some discussion directed toward the abolition of the death penalty altogether, the drafters decided to let it stand as an imposable penalty and prescribe adequate safeguards against executions based

---

231.   The writer regards this as a subtle attempt to side-step the sensitive issue involving the affirmative defense of superior orders which the Allies rejected as being relevant on the merits and admitted such evidence in mitigation and extenuation of the sentence. See Duke, War Crimes, - Obedience to Orders, US Naval Institute Proceedings, p 82 (July 1966).

232.   Thus far, the North Vietnamese and Viet Cong have executed three US Army members, all summary in nature and in total derogation of the GPW. Sergeant Harold G. Bennet was murdered by the Viet Cong in 1965 as revenge for the execution (following a proper trial) of a Viet Cong terrorist. New York Times, p 3, col. 5. Without benefit of a trial, Captain Versace and Sergeant Roraback were murdered by North Viet Nam government in reprisal of the execution of three communists terrorists. 53 State Dept. Bull. 635(1965). Hanoi later acknowledged its responsibility for the execution of Sgt. Bennet as well as the deaths of forty-four persons (including Swiss, US, United Nations, French, and Philippine nationals) at the Saigon restaurant bombing. 53 State Dept. Bull. 55 (1965).

233.   Art. 101, GPW.

on considerations of the moment.[234] The death sentence must be considered by a Board of Review and the Court of Military Appeals before the President can approve and order it executed.[235] In view of the processing time of around 12-18 months from the date sentence is adjudged by the court-martial until action by the Court of Military Appeals, there is no doubt but that the six-month waiting period required by Article 109, GPW, will never be violated by the United States.[236.]

As to other penalties, the Prisoner Convention requires equal treatment of PW's,[237] that there is no deprivation of rank,[238]

---

234. COMMENTARY III 473-5. In enacting the Geneva Convention Act of 1957, the United Kingdom abolished the death penalty for grave breaches and provided for life imprisonment in the event of wilful killing of a PW and 14 years maximum sentence for all other grave breaches. Levie, Penal Sanctions for Maltreatment of Prisoners of War, 56 Am. J. Int'l.L. 433, 455 (fn 90)(1962). From 1930-1965, the US Army carried out 160 executions, of which 148 took place during 1942-50, 3 each in 1954, 1955, and 1957, and one each in 1958, 1959, and 1961. Basis for the executions were murder in one-hundred and six cases (also involving rape) and fifty-three rape cases. The US Navy has not carried out an execution since 1849. NATIONAL PRISONER STATISTICS BULLETIN No. 39, US Bureau of Prisons, p 5(June 1966).

235. Art. 66, 67b(1), and 71(a), UCMJ.

236. An average of 13 months(394 days) processing time was reported for the periods January thru June 1966 and for the month of December 1966 as to contested trials by general courts-martial. Unofficial reports prepared by Records and Analysis Branch, Office of the Judge Advocate General, US Army.

237. Art. 88, GPW.

238. Art. 87; see also COMMENTARY III 432 and 467.

that the prisoner of war remains entitled to the benefits of the Convention at all times,[239] that double jeopardy is a valid defense to a subsequent trial,[240] and that any period of confinement awaiting trial be deducted from the sentence and that the court and reviewing authorities consider such confinement.[241]

The adjudging of forfeitures is authorized under the Prisoner Convention,[242] though resort to such form of punishment seems of dubious effect. In voting on a sentence, the 2/3 rule applies, as in the case of findings,[243] and the method would be by secret written ballot, Where the death sentence is imposable, all members of the court must concur in the punishment.[244]

C. Post-Trial Procedural Matters

Immediately upon the sentence being adjudged by the court, the Protecting Power, prisoners' representative, and the accused are to be notified in writing (in an understandable language) of the sentence.[245] The Protecting Power will also be advised whether

---

239.   Art. 85, GPW.

240.   Art. 86, GPW. This prohibition is applicable not only to the same country's efforts to try the accused a second time, but in the event that the PW is transported to another High Contracting Party under Article 12, GPW, II A, Final Record 501.

241.   Art. 103, GPW.

242.   Art. 87, GPW; paragraph 126h, MCM, 1951.

243.   Art. 51(a), UCMJ.

244.   Art. 52(a)(1), UCMJ.

245.   Art. 107, GPW.

the accused has waived his right to appeal. Where the sentence adjudged is death or where the sentence (in any case) is approved and ordered executed, the United States is to notify the Protecting Power as follows:[246]

    a. forward a copy of the promulgating order;
    b. forward a summarized record of the pre-trial investigation and the trial proceeding (a copy of the post-trial review); and
    c. indicate where the confinement or execution will take place.

Because the prisoner of war has the same right of review as a member of the US armed forces, his case will be reviewed by the Staff Judge Advocate[247] prior to action by the convening authority on the findings and sentence.[248]

A copy of the record of trial, in a language he understands, will be furnished the PW. The defense counsel has benefit of necessary facilities until the term for appeal has expired.[249] The sentence to death cannot be ordered executed until approved by the President after review by a Board of Review and the Court of Military Appeals.

Upon completion of the appellate review set forth in the UCMJ, it is not unlikely that a convicted prisoner of war would seek a writ of habeas corpus from a US federal court. In the leading case regarding the availability of the writ to members of the armed forces to test the conviction by a court-martial, the Supreme Court dismissed without hearing any evidence a petition from two members of the US Air Force convicted of rape and murder at Guam and who

---

246.   ibid.

247.   Art. 61, UCMJ.

248.   Art. 64, UCMJ.

249.   Art. 105, GPW.

alleged denial of due process of law by the military.[250] The
Court re-affirmed its long-standing position that the civil courts
will follow a more narrow ~~narrow~~ scope of review in military habeas
corpus matters because the civil courts are not the proper agencies
to exercise supervision over the military legal system which the
Constitution left to Congress.[251] Upon examination of the record of
trial, the Court found that the petitioners had been accorded a
fair trial by the military system which likewise with the state
courts of the US has a responsibility to ensure against violations
of certain constitutional rights.

In addition to the UCMJ and the writ of habeas corpus, the
PW is also entitled to protection from the Protecting Power which
has a role to play outside the judicial review procedures to ensure
compliance with the GPW. Article 12 provides that in the event of
a dispute as to the interpretation of the Convention, the good
offices of the Protecting Power will be offered in order to resolve
the issue. This is an important procedure for it can serve as the
vehicle for the resolution, at any stage of the judicial process,
of whether a fair trial is being accorded the PW.[252]

---

250.   Burns v Wilson, 346 U.S. 137 (1953)(claimed confessions had
been coerced and counsel of their choice had been denied). For outline on
interrogation of PW's, see Comments, Interrogation under the Prisoner of
War Convention, 21 Mil. L. Rev. 145 (1963).

251.   Fowler v Wilkinson, 353 U.S. 583 (1957), wherein the petitioners
claimed the sentence was arbitrarily severe; Court rejected the contention
declaring that it exercised "no supervisory power of the courts which
enforce military law". See also, U.S. Dep't. of Army Pamphlet 27-174,
Military Justice - Jurisdiction of Courts-Martial (June 1965) for discussion of habeas corpus cases by members of the armed forces, p 20-36.

252.   See section VII - C-4 for additional discussion on point.

VII.

TRIAL OF THE UNLAWFUL BELLIGERENT

A. Procedural Rights Before and During Trial

Unlike the general court-martial trial of the prisoner of war, there is no existing set of rules as such to govern the conduct of the trial by a military commission of the unlawful belligerent. However, the Manual for Courts-Martial, 1951 does provide:[253]

> Subject to any applicable rule of international law or to any Regulation prescribed by the President or by other competent authority, these tribunals (military commissions and provost courts) will be guided by the applicable principles of law and rules of procedure and evidence prescribed by courts-martial.

Identical provisions are found in both the 1921 and 1928 Manual for Courts-Martial (the latter was applicable until 1949), but the issuance by the President of Executive Orders creating Military Commissions during and after WW II allowed these tribunals to apply rules different than those applicable in courts-martials. General Yamashita, when tried before a US Army military commission in Manila for pre-capture offenses agianst the law of war, claimed that as a prisoner of war, he was entitled to the benefits of the Articles of War and should therefore have been tried before a court-martial and that evidence of a probative value should not have been admissable in his trial which resulted in conviction and imposition

---

253.   p 1, paragraph 2.

of the death sentence.[254] Although today that case would have been tried before a general court-martial, the rule of that case is legally applicable to the trial of an unlawful belligerent before a military commission. The US Supreme Court was thus squarely faced with the proper standard of due process applicable. Two Justices felt that the due process clause of the Fifth Amendment of the Constitution extended to everyone accused of a crime by the United States Government and to make an exception in the case of enemy belligerents was "contrary to the whole philosophy of human rights."[255] But, the majority of the Court regarded international law was (a) dispositive of the issue and (b) provided the proper standard of due process of law. The distinguished professor of International Law, Quincy Wright, reviewed this holding quite extensively and found it to be in accord with the principle of a fair trial as required by international law. He points out that the accused was not denied justice in the sense that there was a denial of those rights regarded as indispensible to the proper administration of justice, although he considers that the accused should have been given additional time to prepare for the defense of his case.[256] Thus, due process, it must be remembered, does

---

254. _In re Yamashita_, 327 U.S. 1, 18-20. In that case, the Supreme Court found that Congress, by adding concurrent jurisdiction in AW 15, sanctioned the commission and permitted to the President "any use of the military commission contemplated by the common law of war," and also found not restriction on its procedures. p 20. An interesting account of the trial and appeal is presented by the US Army defense counsel in Reel, THE CASE OF GENERAL YAMASHITA (1949)

255. _supra_ note 254 at 79.

256. Due Process and International Law, 40 Am. J. Int'l. L. 398, 406 (1946).

not require any particular type of treatment so long as the proceedings afford the accused an impartial hearing and adequate safeguards for the protection of individual rights.[257]

The Supreme Court found in the Yamashita case that the proceedings by the military commission conformed with the internatinal law standard of due process and a fair trial. The balance of thies section deals with the specific elements of the WW II proceedings before such tribunals and outline any changes which may have evolved in international law since that time, and which would be applicable under Article 3 of the Civilian Convention.

Before delving into a detailed analysis of the provisions of the Conventions and other references to determine the components of procedural safeguards for a fair trial of the unlawful belligerent under Art 3, GC, the following quotation should be kept in mind:[258]

> He that would make his own liberty secure must guard even his enemy from oppression, for if he violates this duty he establishes a precedent that will reach even himself.

257. In 1931, the Chief Justice, speaking for the majority, held that the Congress, in exercising its authority to alter or revise the maritime law of the US, had provided a procedure before an administrative official for the determination of compensable injuries which did not violate the due process clause of the Fifth Amendment, in Crowell v Benson, 285 U.S. 22. Also, Justice Holmes, speaking for the majority, rejected a claim by one imprisoned for 2 and 1/2 months by order of the Adjutant General of a state national guard during an insurrection in Colorado and declared: "But it is familiar that what is due process of law depends on the circumstances. It varies with the subject matter and the necessities of the situation. Moyer v Peabody, 212 U.S. 78, 84 (1909). See also Forencz, Nuremberg Trial Procedure and the Rights of the Accused, 39 J. Crim. L. Rev. 145 (1948).

258. Tom Paine, quoted by Brooks, THE WORLD OF WASHINGTON IRVING 73.

1. WW II Proceedings - Brief Review

The first proceedings conducted by a United States military Commission during World War II took place in Washington, DC in the summer of 1942 and concerned eight German soldiers (one of whom claimed to be a US citizen) who landed at two locations along the Eastern seaboard of the United States in military uniform for the purpose of conducting sabotage activities against defense installations for which they had been trained in Berlin. They burned their uniforms after landing ashore and were taken into custody while proceeding to the target installations. Acting under Article 38 of the Articles of War (forerunner of today's Article 36 of the UCMJ), the President prescribed in an Executive Order the establishment of a military commission for the trial of these unlawful combatants. The commission consisted of seven general officers and the trial was prosecuted by the Judge Advocate General of the Army. Rules of procedure and evidence were to be prescribed by the commission and the Executive Order authorized the receipt into evidence of all evidence of a probative value. A full and fair hearing was to be accorded the accused and a 2/3 vote was required as to all issues, including findings and sentence.

On application for a writ of habeas corpus to the US Supreme Court, it was held that the action of the President in establishing the military commission and granting it the above guidance should "not be set aside by the courts without the clear conviction that

---

259.   Infra, note 205.

his action was in conflict with the Constitution or laws of Congress constitutionally enacted." In dismissing the assertion of entitlement to trial by jury and other guarantees of the Constitution, the Court found no such conflict here.[260]

In this manner, the stage was set for a lengthy procession of cases tried before military commissions, either of an international or national character, in which judicial review was rejected on the ground that the entire proceeding in each case was a proper exercise of jurisdiction which did not exceed its authorized bounds.

The next major judicial proceeding against war criminals took place in Nuremberg, Germany before the International Military Tribunal which sat in judgment of twenty-four of the leading Nazis and six Nazi organizations from October 1945 until October of the following year. The tribunal had been established by the Charter created by the Allied Powers and set forth the principle that the accused were to receive a fair trial and in particular: to receive a copy of the indictment and all documents pertaining to their case; to be present during any preliminary investigation; to be furnished copies of documents which were to be translated into a language understood by the accused; to have a choice of defense counsel or the accused could defend himself; and to present evidence and call witnesses.[261] Although this case failed to receive judicial review by any national court, few prominent international law publicists,

a _____

260.   Ex parte Quirin, 317 U.S. 1 (1943)

261.   For text of the London Agreement and the Charter, see 13 State Dept. Bull. 222 (1945).

aside from other misgivings falling into the policy considerations

of conducting such a trial, asserted that the procedural aspects

of the case resulted in a denial of justice.[262]   The same procedure

was followed before the I.M.T. for the Far East sitting in Tokyo,

the Subsequent Proceedings at Nuremberg, the Military Government

Courts at Dachau, the military commissions at Yokohama and

elsewhere involving the United States.

2. Appointing Authority

The initial trials of war criminals by the United States

involved the appointment of military commissions at the personal

direction of the President. After the termination of hostilities

in 1945, the President delegated the appointing authority to the

major field commanders and at one time appointing authority extended

---

262.   Schwartzenberger, The Trial at Nuremberg, 21 Tul. L. Rev.,
329 (1947); Biddle, The Nuremberg Trial, 33 Va. L. Rev. 679 (1947)
(Mr. Biddle was the Attorney General and assisted in the prosecution
of the Quirin case and was a judge from the United States on the
I.M.T. at Nuremberg); Q. Wright, The Law of the Nuremberg Trial,
41 Am. J. Int'l. L. 38, 51 (1947); where there was denial of justice
or an appearance thereof, prompt action was taken to remedy the
situation, as in the case of the Malmedy Massacre, United States v
Bersin) wherein the Germans conducted mass murder of US PW's
incident to the Battle of the Bulge; upon capture, the responsible
parties were subject to mock trials in an effort by the US to secure
confessions from appointed "defense counsels"; The US Supreme Court
rejected writ of habeas corpus, several investigations were conducted
including one by the Senate, and General Clay finally commuted six
of the death sentences (out of forty-three originally adjudged) to
life, and allowed six other death sentences to be carried out on
a finding that the pre-trial investigation had not prejudiced the
six death sentences; see Koessler, Review and Investigation Odyssey
in the Malmedy Massacre Case, 6 Crim. L. Rev. 39 (1959).

to the field army commander.[263]   There is no written authority

for the proposition that the President must appoint or delegate

his appointing authority, but the practice to this effect has arisen

and is binding today.

Under the National Security Act of 1947, as amended, there

are now seven unified and one specified combatant commands responsible

to the Joint Chiefs of Staff[264] and it is proper for these commanders

to be delegated the authority to appoint military commissions and

to re-delegate such appointing authority.

3. Composition

Generally, three to five officers were appointed to serve

as members of the commission, the senior member being designated

as President. Although challenges for cause were not generally

permitted under either the American or British system during

World War II,[265] such challenges must be permitted in order to

---

263.   Koessler, American War Crimes Trials in Europe, 39 Geo. L. J.
18, 34 (1950). In the Yamashita case, the President directed the Joint
Chiefs of Staff to instruct General MacArthur, Commander-in-Chief, US
Army Forces, Pacific, to proceed with the trials of war criminals; in
turn, Lieutenant General Styer, Commanding General, US Army Forces,
Western Pacific, was directed to proceed with the trial of General
Yamashita; 327 U.S. 5, 10-11. In the same manner, the military
commission in the Eisentrager case was established by the Commanding
General, US Forces at Nanking after he received authorization from the
Joint Chiefs of Staff through the Commanding General, US Forces, China
Theater; 339 U.S. 763, 766.

264.   10 USC § 124 (1962)(PL 89-651) The unified commands are:
Europe, Pacific, Atlantic, Southern,Alaskan, Continental Air, and
Strike. The specified command is the Strategic Air Command. The
Adjutant General's School, Memorandum 202-1, Organization of the Depart-
ment of Defense p 13 (April 1966).

265.   Article II (e), Ordinance No. 7, promulgated under Control
Council Law No. 10 for the trial by the US at Dachau contained a

ensure a fair and impartial tribunal and that the accused has the
opportunity to raise any grounds for bias and other factors at
the trial level and place the matter in the record for appellate
consideration.[266]

Several of the Allies permitted foreign officers to serve
as members of their commission, but the United States did not
during WW II.[267] It is regarded the better practice to exclude
from membership foreign officers because they might feel under an
obligation to vote in favor of conviction and a severe sentence.

The members of the military commission should be where
possible senior in grade to the accused,[268] and free from all

---

prohibition against challenges by the accused against either the
tribunal or its members; Appendix L, Taylor, FINAL REPORT 286 (1949).

266.   The Yokahama trials proved to be the exception as to allowing challenges for cause against members of the US Army military
commission because in the first such trial, the accused's challenge
against a member on grounds he had been a Japanese PW in the Philippines was sustained; Spurlock, The Yokahama War Trials, 36 A.B.A.J.
387, 388(1950). Professor L.C. Green regards the impartiality of the
tribunal as one of the most important components of a fair trial, see
Legal Issues in the Eichmann Trial, 37 Tul. L. Rev. 641(1963). Snee
and Pye conclude that a fair and impartial tribunal is also implicitly
required and that challenges be allowed so as to ensure a fair trial
for the accused; Due Process in Criminal Procedure: A Comparison of
Two Systems, 21 Ohio State L. J. 467, 496-7 (1960).

267.   For example, French officers sat as members of a British
military court in Germany involving the death of French nationals, as
reported in 5 LAW REPORTS, 39(1948). Article V of the British Royal
Warrant allowed for Mixed Inter-Allied Courts, see 4 LAW REPORTS 127 for text.

268.   The objection by a German Lieutenant General being tried
before a US Army military commission composed of officers of lesser
rank was rejected where he requested officers senior in grade to
serve as commission members, United States v Laelzer, as reported
in 11 LAW REPORTS 53 (1949).

command influence.

4. The Law Member

None of the Allied tribunals in the 1940's had an officer to serve apart from the tribunal and advise it on legal matters, these duties normally were performed by the Trial Judge Advocate (prosecutor). The two I.M.T's consisted of jurists from several countries, the Subsequent Proceedings at Nuremberg had as judges members from various state courts, but other tribunals involving the US lacked the services of attorneys, except for counsel. The United Nations' Command rules for military commission, dated 28 October 1950, provided for the appointment of a five-member commission with a Law Member to be from the Judge Advocate General's Corps to serve as legal advisor and vote with the commission,[269] a practice followed by the British military courts in the trial of WW II war criminals.

There is no mention among the reported cases or writings that international law requires a judge to preside over the trial of an alien and a fortori a war criminal. Although, under Article 3 of the Civilian Convention there is no duty to appoint a trial judge, it would serve the interests of justice to do so and have him discharge his duties to advise the commission on matters of law. The Law Member should not vote with the commission nor otherwise participate in their closed deliberations.

---

269. Rule 6c, of order entitled Trial of Accused War Criminals, issued by General Headquarters, United Nations Command, AG 000.5 (hereinafter referred to as UNC Procedure.)

5. Defense Counsel

Customary international law quite clearly provides for the services of an attorney to assist the accused, or at least that the accused be afforded the opportunity to have these services. The Declaration of Human Rights, the Prisoner Convention, the Civilian Convention provisions relating to occupation, all refer to the requirement of a defense counsel to assist the accused. Prior to these pronouncements, counsel had been provided by the Allies during the trial of the WW II war crimes and denial of counsel to Allied prisoners of war during their trials served as the basis of charges of violations of the law of war against those enemy personnel responsible for such denial.[270]

Before the I.M.T. in Nuremberg, German attorneys (often times former members of the Nazi party themselves) served as counsel for the accused, and this practice was followed before the Subsequent Proceedings.[271] The other trials conducted by the United States, however, found American military attorneys serving as defense counsel. The UN Command would have restricted the appointment of counsel to those members of the bar of any nation which was a member of the United Nations.[272] Such a restriction is untenable and the accused's choice of counsel should remain unfettered, subject to curtailment only on the basis of security considerations.

---

270.   Supra note 23.

271.   Taylor, FINAL REPORT 297.

272.   Rule 32, UNC Procedure.

In the event of rejection of requested counsel, the record should reflect the reasons therefor.

6. Admissibility of Evidence

Under the heading of a fair and full hearing required by international law, there appears to be no objection to the civil law system rule that all evidence of probative value be admitted and that the triers of the fact are to attach weight thereto. This practice was followed by the United States WW II war crimes trials and was not found to be objectionable by the US Supreme Court.[273] This rule allowing evidence of probative value results in the admission in capital cases of depositions, diaries, hearsay and evidence of a similar nature, subject to the accused's ability to refute it and the weight to be attached to such evidence by the military commission.

General Yamashita objected to the introduction of depositions, hearsay evidence and the like at his trial which resulted in the death sentence. The Supreme Court ruled that since he was not subject to the Articles of War and since the President had permitted evidence of probative value to be admitted, there was no prohibition to the receipt of this evidence. This ruling is consistent with the international law standard of due process and it is proper for the President to exercise his authority and change the rule in the Manual for Courts-Martial, 1951, which now bars this type of evidence in a trial before a military commission.

---

273.   In re Yamashita, 327 U.S. 1, 20(1946). In evaluating the US trials, Professor Forencz states that there was no denial of

Although the deposition involved in the trial by a general court-martial requires that the accused and his counsel be present at the taking thereof,[274] no such requirement exists under international law and it is permissible to secure testimony from an absent witness under an order of the tribunal and where the testimony is taken under oath.

Professor Quincy Wright adds that international tribunals as well as courts in most civil law countries admit such evidence.[275] This procedure can be tailored to the military commission proceeding through instructions by the Law Member who would rule on the proffered

---

justice or deprivation of a fair trial because of the probative value rule; in fact, the accused made use of this evidentiary rule more than the prosecution, supra note 257 at 148.

274.   Art. 49d, UCMJ.

275.   War Criminals, 39 Am. J. Int'l. L. 257, 285 (1945), and Due Process and International Law, 40 Am. J. Intl. L. 398, 404-5 (1946). Art. 72, GC assures that protected persons "shall have the right to present evidence necessary to their defense..." Pictet indicates that the drafters wanted to show "clearly that the accused may use all other methods of proof such as the production of documents or other written evidence." COMMENTARY IV 356. The US has recently enacted legislation permitting assistance of US district courts in gathering evidence in criminal, as well as civil, cases before foreign courts and international tribunals. Prior to enactment of 28 USC § 1782 in 1964, the existing legislation permitted assistance only in civil cases. (In re Letter Rogatory, 26 F. Supp. 852 (D.C. Md. 1939) where Baltimore court refused to assist in murder trial pending in Versailles, France.) Thus, the US will give assistance to a system of law allowing admission of matters with probative value. Legislative history of this Act is found in 2 CONGRESSIONAL AND ADMINISTRATIVE NEWS 3782, 3784-5 (1964). For the practice as used by British Commonwealth military tribunals, see Dunn, Trial of War Criminals, 19 Aust. L. J. 359(1946), for comparison of US authority and British Royal Charter provisions.

testimony's possession of probative value, then instruct the members of the commission of their duty to attach whatever weight they deemed appropriate in order to establish the truth of the matter in issue.

7. Calling Witnesses

The standard of a fair trial under Article 3 of the Civilian Convention requires that the accused have the right to call witnesses. Every effort must be made to allow the accused to produce necessary witnesses and produce relevant evidence on his behalf.

It would be proper for the tribunal to appoint commissioners for the purpose of taking evidence from distant witnesses, a practice followed by the United States in the Subsequent Proceedings at Nuremberg.[276] The accused is to be afforded every opportunity to locate and interview material witnesses in order to exercise fully his rights in this regard under the Civilian Convention. Where the witness in question is or may himself become the accused in a criminal proceeding should he personally appear, the accused would be required to secure his testimony by means of an affidavit or similar writing, because involuntary self-incrimination is not permitted. The same would hold true for the prosecution, but would be limited (if at all applicable) to rebutting matters in extenuation and mitigation.

The problem of reluctant witnesses confronted Eichmann during his trial in 1962 in Tel Aviv, Israel. His able defense counsel, Dr. Servatius, objected to the court for the failure of the

---

276.   Taylor, FINAL REPORT 89-90.

prosecution to grant safe conduct to only those defense witnesses not wanted by the State of Israel and thus excluding many witnesses who were then wanted by the authorities or might be through their testimony from the witness stand. The court overruled the objection, stating that secondary evidence was the proper method of presenting this testimony.[277] Where it is necessary for the defense counsel or his associates to travel into areas frequently subject to hostile actions or to countries not recognized diplomatically by the United States, every effort must be made by the U.S. to facilitate the necessary travel in order to secure the testimony from essential witnesses.[278]

8. Trial in Absentia

Can an unlawful belligerent be tried in absentia, as in the case where he has fled the country and extradition or other means to secure custody are futile? Although Martin Borman's defense counsel's motion to bar trial on the ground that he was not present before the International Military Tribunal at Nuremberg was overruled and Borman was convicted and sentenced to

---

277. Green, Legal Issues in the Eichmann Trial, 37 Tul.L. Rev. 641, 655 (1963). For a general account of the trial from the prosecutor's vantage point, see Hauser JUDGMENT IN JERUSALEM (1966).

278. The United States was not only required to validate a passport to Communist Red China and North Korea, but also finance the travel of the defense counsel in 1958 for the purpose of taking depositions from known individuals incident to a sedition trial. United States v Powell et al, 156 F. Supp. 526 (ND Cal, 1957).

death,[279] such a proceeding has validity today under international law.[280] Some of the civil law countries permit trials _in absentia_ in criminal cases, but, as in the case of Germany, it is often restricted to nationals and there is every effort to allow for the re-opening of the case upon good cause when the convicted person returns to the jurisdiction of the court.[281] Also, the United States insists that persons extradited from the US be given a new trial in those cases where a trial in absentia has been conducted by the requesting government.[282]

---

279.   22 THE TRIAL OF MAJOR WAR CRIMINALS 528(1951). The defense counsel, Fredrich Bergold, objected to the trial of his absent client. Two questions linger regarding Borman: is he alive and if so, what should be done with him in the event his whereabouts becomes known. As to the first, there is much speculation. As to the second question, there are two courses of action open: a) return Borman to the Control Council for appropriate action under Article 29 of the I.M.T. Charter which empowered this agency to carry out the judgments of the Tribunal (it could nullify the judgment and release Borman to another state for trial, or modify the sentence to imprisonment for life or a term of years or b) release him to a requesting state for prosecution on the same charges as were before the I.M.T., in whole or in part, or on new charges (if possible). It is submitted that the better choice lies in the second alternative.

280.   The Anglo-American rule is traced to the power of the court to enforce its judgment once rendered but today's concept of presence at trial is so rooted in fairness, that trial _in absentia_ appears to be vanishing from the scene. Snee & Pye, _supra_ note 266 at 485-8.

281.   Art. 277 of the German Criminal Code allows trial _in absentia_; Art. 14 provides for maximum punishment as life imprisonment, capital punishment having been abolished. 4 THE AMERICAN SERIES OF FOREIGN PENAL CODES (1961).

282.   _Galinna v Fraser_, 177 F. Supp. 856 (DC Conn. 1959), holds that it is not contrary to due process to extradite a person, even where the accused might not receive a new trial, the first one having been _in absentia_.

9. Copy of the Charges & Trial Preparation

The accused and his counsel, at the first opportunity, should be furnished with a copy of the charges and allied papers in a language which they understand. Adequate time to prepare for the case must be allowed by the appointing authority.[283]

10. Voting

The rulings and judgments by the two I.M.T.'s were by way of majority vote, but the other war crimes trials involving the United States followed the 2/3 rule as to all issues, including findings and sentence. The UN Command proposed a voting scheme which should be adopted by the military commission in future trials, namely: 2/3 vote on all questions, including findings and sentence, except that in capital cases a 3/4 vote was required as to findings and sentence.[284] There is no requirement under international law that a certain vote is required in order to have a valid conviction and punishment.

---

283.   Although Article 3, GC, is aimed only at summary judgment (COMMENTARY IV 39), the accused is entitled to know of the charges against him and to have adequate time in which to prepare his defense. Several of the cases prosecuted by the US were on charges that the accused failed to allow the victims to prepare for their trials. 5 LAW REPORTS 1, 60, 466 (1948). General MacArthur ordered new trials in two instances wherein the prosecution failed to translate classified documents for the accused. Spurlock, supra note 266 at 389.

284.   Rule 35, UNC Procedure.

B. Sentencing Power

Sentencing power of the military commission consists of
two topics: what punishments are imposable and how can they be
imposed. Historically, the military commission has enjoyed unlimited
power in regards to the imposition of punishments. Colonel Winthrop
reports that the commission is not limited as in the case of the
courts-martial and that its punishments include: death, imprisonment,
and fine, plus indemnification for property stolen, restoration,
confiscation and even required to pay the costs of the prosecution.
During the War Between the States, the military commission would
often banish or expel the accused, or impose internment.[285]

The trials conducted before the I.M.T.'s, the Subsequent
Proceedings, and the other trials of war criminals were guided by
the principle that the punishment should be suited to the crime.[286]
Great flexibility was granted the US military commission in
imposing death or lesser punishments of imprisonment. The authority
to impose these punishments as well as confiscation and restoration
in appropriate cases should be carried forward into future trials.

On the matter of voting, the military commission has
traditionally used the 2/3 rule in order to convict and to sentence.
This rule was applicable to all US war crimes proceedings following
World War II, except the two I.M.T.'s where a majority vote controlled
as to the imposition of punishment. A dramatic contrast in the area

---

285.   WINTHROP 842-4.

286.   Control Council Law No. 10 appearing in both 15 State Dept.
Bull. 862(1946) and Taylor, FINAL REPORT 250-1(1949); see also Articles
26 and 28, I.M.T. Charter, 13 State Dept. Bull. 222 (1945).

of voting exists when one compares the 2/3 rule to impose the death sentence on the unlawful belligerent for commission of a capital offense, whereas the prisoner of war must be found guilty as well as sentenced by a general court-martial by a unanimous vote.

The UN Command's proposed voting scheme called for a 2/3 vote on findings and sentence as to non-capital offenses and 3/4 vote as to capital cases.[287] This voting procedure is submitted as the better approach.

During the Second World War war crimes trials, the common law countries followed the practice of merely announcing the findings and sentences without comment, whereas the civil law countries accompanied their decisions with written justification for their conclusions. The international law standard of due process does not require reasons for the findings or sentence and the US tribunals should not do so.

C. Post-Trial Procedural Matters

1. Review by Military Authorities

Acting under the Article 3 standard of due process to ensure a fair trial, there is absolutely no requirement to review or to allow appeal from the decision of the tribunal in the event of conviction in order to execute it.[288] However, the practice

---

287.   Rule 35, UNC Procedure.

288.   Thus, the proposed International Criminal Court (in Art. 50) expressly stated that there would be no appeals from convictions. Text of the draft statute contained in 40 Am. J. Int'l. L. Supp. 1(1952). Appraisal of the post-WW II emergence of judicial review in Europe appears in Dietze, Judicial Review in Europe, 55 Mich. L. Rev. 539 (1957).

within the US Army has been for the appointing authority, at least, to review the commission's action and then order the sentence into execution. Colonel Winthrop refers to the action of the reviewing or appointing officer being much wider in the case of a military commission than in a court-martial case, in that the sentence of the commission can be changed by making the punishment less severe, such as changing imprisonment to release of the accused upon a pledge of good behavior or legal conduct in the future, in addition to the normal powers to approve, disapprove or remit the punishment.[290]

Various methods of review were followed by the US Army incident to the World War II trials, ranging from approval by the President in the Quirin case to the approval by the field commanders in Germany in those cases tried under Control Council Law Number 10.[1] The two I.M.T.'s were reviewed by the Control Council as to the Nuremberg proceedings and by the Supreme Allied Commander as to the Far East proceedings, there being no provision for appeal in either of these proceedings. However, petitions for clemency were allowed by the Control Council.

In addition to action by an appointing authority, there was a higher level of command which exercised reviewing power as to all other cases tried by the United States. The Subsequent Proceedings at Nuremberg and the trials conducted at Dachau under Control Council Law Number 10 were forwarded to the US Military

---

290.   Koessler, supra note 263.

291.   [illegible]

Governor of the US Zone of Occupation who, as the reviewing authority, exercised the power to mitigate, reduce, or otherwise alter the sentence, subject to the prohibition against increasing it. The Dachau trials were reviewed by the judge advocates on the staff of the appointing authorities (the Commanding Generals of the 3rd and 8th Armies) who then took action which was final on all cases, except those involving the death sentence which were forwarded to the theater commander for his approval. In addition, there was appointed by the theater commander in 1950 a War Crimes Modification Board to handle the matter of leniency. This was necessary because the severity of the sentences became less and less as the years passed and there was a need to adjust the sentences.[291]

The UN Command provided for review by the Supreme Allied Commander in capital cases and the action by the appointing authority in all other cases was final.[292]

Where the United States conducts war crimes trials in the future, there should be uniform military review procedures under which the field army appointing authority is granted final review powers on all findings and sentences not extending to death, in which case the record of trial must be acted upon by the theater commander. A War Crimes Modification Board should be created to review all sentences to consider clemency matters.

---

291.   Koessler, supra note 263 at 92. See also Taylor, FINAL REPORT 90-93.

292.   Rule 40, UNC Procedure.

2. Judicial Review

Should the proceedings before a military commission be reviewable by a US court? The Supreme Court answered this question in the negative when many of those convicted by such tribunals sought petitions for leave to file motions for writs of habeas corpus. In the first case to come before it, the Supreme Court in the Quirin case dismissed the petition upon its finding that the commission was properly constituted and that the tribunal did not deny the accused a fair trial. This case takes on added significance as to the lack of the right to obtain judicial review when one considers that the trial took place in Washington, D.C. at a time when civilian courts were open and functioning. The Court was quick to cast aside an attempt by the President in his Proclamation to foreclose the courts from reviewing this case,[293] since, as the majority reasoned, this did not "preclude access to the courts for determining its applicability to the particular case."[294]

There were no other US trials of war crime offenses during the war, but after the war most every person convicted by US tribunals sought judicial review of decisions rendered by tribunals established by the US acting alone or jointly with other nations.[295] The first such case involved General Yamashita who

---

293.   7 Fed. Reg. 5101 (1942).

294.   317 U.S. 1, 25 (1942).

295.   Footnote 1 of the decision in Hirota v MacArthur, 335 U.S. 876(1948) lists the many cases in which judicial review had been sought; see also footnote 1 of the Eisentrager case, supra note 263 at 767 for additional cases.

asserted, _inter alia,_ that the denial of certain basic rights thereby deprived the military commission of jurisdiction to try him and that habeas corpus was the only method by which he could test the findings and sentence. The Supreme Court denied the petition, holding that the petitioner had been accorded a fair trial, in that no command of the Constitution, statute, or military command had been violated.[296.] This case was decided in February 1946 and it was not for another two years that the Court decided another war crimes trial when it considered the challenge of the proceedings before the I.M.T. for the Far East.

In this period of time, however, many of those convicted at Nuremberg in the twelve Subsequent Proceedings applied to the U.S. Supreme Court for the issuance of the writ of habeas corpus, but all such requests were denied in Memorandum opinions indicating a lack of jurisdiction in the Court to consider the cases. The Justices were divided four to four, with Mr. Justice Jackson taking no part in the case arising in Germany because of his work as Chief Prosecutor before the I.M.T. at Nuremberg and in creating Control Council Law Number 10 on which all the other cases in Germany were based.

However, when the case from the Far East tribunal came to the Court on a request to file a petition, Mr. Jackson decided to vote in favor of granting a hearing to this great issue before the Nation. In casting his vote as he did, he carefully pointed out his position and declared his feeling that a hearing must be granted to

---

296.   327 U.S. 1 (1946).

bring the matter into the open in view of the equal division of the Court and because the four who favored the hearing of the German cases had taken their opinions out of conference and to the public.[297]

The day after hearing argument the Court handed down a per curiam opinion in which the petition was denied. The Supreme Court considered that the International Military Tribunal for the Far East was not a tribunal of the United States, but rather an international tribunal established by General MacArthur as the Supreme Allied Commander for the Allied Powers. In view of the international nature of the tribunal, "...the courts of the United States have no power or authority to review, to affirm, set aside or annul the judgments and sentences imposed..."[298]

As in the Yamashita case, Justices Murphy and Rutledge dissented but filed no opinion. Justice Jackson took no part in the decision. Justice Douglas concurred in the result only because the tribunal was not a court but was rather "an instrument of military power". He would have granted the District Court jurisdiction to examine the cause of the restraint of liberty and he would not deny the writ of habeas corpus where an officer of the United States was concerned, even though he was acting in the capacity as a member of an international command. To quote from

_____

297.   335 U.S. 876 (1948).

298.   338 U.S. 107, 199 (1949).

his opinion:

> The conclusion is therefore plain that the Tokyo Tribunal acted as an instrument of military power of the Executive Branch of Government. It responded to the will of the Supreme Allied Commander as expressed in the military order by which he constituted it. It took its laws from its creator and did not act as a free and independent tribunal to adjudge the rights of the petitioners under international law....Insofar as American participation is concerned, there is no constitutional objection. For the capture and control of those who were responsible for the Pearl Harbor incident was a political question on which the President as Commander-in-Chief, and as spokesman for the nation in foreign affairs, had the final say. (at p 215)

On the basis of the _Hirota_ case, the Court of Appeals for the District of Columbia dismissed a grant of the writ of habeas corpus by a lower court in a case arising from the Subsequent Proceedings, entitled _Flick v Johnson_. This holding by the Court of Appeals traced the developments leading up to the enactment of the Control Council Law Number 10 and found that since the tribunal which tried the petitioners had this law as its source of jurisdiction, it was an international tribunal over which the national courts were barred from exercising power.[299] The petitioners had urged that the tribunal was in fact national in nature and had been illegally constituted. The Supreme Court denied certiorari.[300]

Should the South Viet-Nam government and its five allies providing military forces agree to punish violators of the laws of war, establish a Central Council for the Prosecution of War

---

299.   174 F. 2d 983 (DC Cir. 1949) and also reported in 3 TRIALS, styled _United States v Flick_.

300.   338 U.S. 879 (1949) and Note, 59 Yale L. Rev. 997 (1950).

Criminals which authorizes the member states to conduct trials, and the US then prosecute war crimes before military commissions, it is submitted that the proceedings of this nature would be international in nature and thus definitely beyond the reach of the US courts should efforts be made to seek judicial review.

The final World War II war crimes case to be decided by the US Supreme Court involved the trial by a US Army military commission of twenty-one German nationals on breaches of the surrender agreement. The accused continued to gather military intelligence data for the Japanese regarding US troops activities in China after the surrender of Germany in May 1945. They were considered military personnel and tried before a commission appointed by the Commanding General, US Army Nanking Headquarters Command, in August 1945. They were found guilty and sentenced to imprisonment which was carried out in the Landsberg Prison where they were placed in the custody of the Commanding General, Third US Army after their repatriation to Germany.[301]

The petition, filed with the District Court in Washington, D.C., was dismissed because the petitioners were never within the territory of the court.[302] The Court of Appeals, however, reversed

---

301.   United States v Eisentrager, as reported in 14 LAW REPORTS 8 (1949).

302.   The statutory authority for the issuance of a writ of habeas corpus then, as now, appears in 28 USC § 2246 which provides, in part, that a prisoner is entitled to a writ where (a) he is in custody under or by color of the authority of the United States or is committed for trial before some US court, or (b) he is a citizen of a foreign country, who is in custody for an act done under the authority of any foreign state. The purpose of the writ is to inquire into the legality of detention of one in custody. Heflin v United States, 358 U.S. 415 (1959).

the dismissal on the theory that "...any person who is deprived of his liberty by officials of the United States, acting under purported authority of that Government, and who can show that his confinement is in violation of a prohibition of the Constitution, has a right to the writ." In following along the theme of Mr. Justice Douglas in the Hirota case, the Court of Appeals based its position on these elements: (1) the Fifth Amendment's due process phrase applies to "any person", (2) where the Government action is in violation of the Constitution, it is void, (3) the judicial branch has the power to examine all acts of the government to ensure compliance with the Constitution and (4) the writ of habeas corpus is the "time-honored" process to test government action affecting personal liberty. Moreover, at the time of the decision, the Supreme Court had ruled that the district court must hear writ of habeas corpus proceedings on the basis of testimony from witnesses present in court and that depositions or other ex parte statements or affidavits were improper.[303]

On certiorari, the Supreme Court reversed the Court of Appeals and dismissed the petition, holding that non-resident alien enemies are not embraced by the Constitutional guarantees of the country against whom they have taken arms, and thus could not bring habeas corpus actions in the courts of the United States.[304] The decision was 6-3, with Mr. Justice Black, with whom Justices

---

303.   174 F. 2d 961 (DC Cir. 1949).

304.   339 U.S. 763 (1950).

Douglas and Burton concurred, dissenting.

The Court based its denial of the writ on the ground that the petitioners had never been within the United States and were alien enemies. The Court also maintained the distinction between lawful and unlawful combatant. Speaking for the majority, Mr. Justice Jackson stated:[305]

> To grant the writ to those prisoners might mean that our army must transport them across the seas for hearings ...This might also require transportation for whatever witnesses the prisoner desired to call as well as transportation for those necessary to defend legality of the sentence. The writ, since it is held to be a matter of right, would be equally available to enemies during hostilities as in the present twilight war and peace. Such trials would hamper the war effort and bring aid and comfort to the enemy. They would diminish the prestige of our commanders, not only with enemies but with wavering neutrals. It would be difficult to devise more effective fettering of a field commander than to allow the very enemy he is ordered to reduce to submission to call him to account in his own civil courts and divert his efforts and attention from the military offensive abroad to the legal defense at home.

The Court then proceeded to demonstrate the error committed by the Circuit Court in granting extra-territorial application of this important procedural right, and concluded that: "When we analyze the claim prisoners are asserting and the court below sustained, it amounts to a right not to be tried at all for an offense against our armed forces. If the Fifth Amendment protects

---

305.   Supra note 304 at 777-8. At the time of this decision, the Supreme Court had ruled in Walker v Johnson, 312 U.S. 284 (1941), that ex parte statements were improper evidence during writ of habeas corpus cases; however, this ruling was changed by 28 USC § 2246 (1964) which permits the use of oral or deposition evidence, or even affidavits, if the trial judge so orders.

them from military trial, the Sixth Amendment clearly prohibits their trial by the civil courts."

It is not that the civil rights group of Amendments contain no limitations as to territory or persons, but the Court refused to adopt the construction below which would "mean that during military occupation irreconcilable enemy elements, guerrilla fighters, and 'werewolves' could require the American judiciary to assure their freedoms of speech, press, and assembly...right to bear arms... security against unreasonable search and seizure...as well as rights to jury trials."[306]

Moving on to the second and third points of the Circuit Court's decision, Justice Jackson held that the military commission has jurisdiction to punish those guilty of offenses against the law of war and, relying on Yamashita, stated that the sole function of the court is to determine the lawful power of the commission and that there was no showing here that it acted in excess of its lawful powers.

In his dissent, Justice Black agreed fully with the Circuit Court's extension of the habeas corpus jurisdiction to alien enemies for the limited purpose of determining whether the military commission was "legally constituted and whether it had jurisdiction to impose the punishment for the conduct charged."[307]

In summary, the Supreme Court's position has been uniformly

---

306.   *Supra* note 304 at 784.

307.   *Supra* note 304 at 797.

to deny petitions for writs of habeas corpus arising from war crimes trials on the grounds that either the tribunal in question was international in nature or that the petitioner was not entitled to such a writ. In denying the entitlement to the writ, the Court has addressed itself to both the in-country and out of country situs regarding trial and confinement. In each case, it is noted that the Court assured itself that the military commission had jurisdiction over the subject matter and the accused, that a fair trial was conducted, and an otherwise legal sentence was imposed, thereby achieving indirectly what it pretends not to have the power to do directly, while maintaining at all times that the Constitution does not follow the flag in such situations.[308]

The last case in point of time to raise the issue of war crimes trials before the federal courts is the 1956 decision from the 10th Circuit, upholding the trial by military commission on charges that the accused passed through the military lines of the United States for the purpose of spying during November 1944 on behalf of the Third Reich, appearing in civilian attire for purposes of espionage and conspiracy to commit these offenses. Under the same Presidential Proclamation in the Quirin case, the President charged the accused with violating the law of war and directed the Commanding General, Second Service Command to convene a military commission for trial. The accused applied

---

308. Fairman, Some New Problems of the Constitution Following the Flag, 1 Stan. L. 587 (1949); Note, 44 Mich. L. Rev. 855 (1946).

for a writ of habeas corpus some time after his conviction, alleging that he was triable only by the civil courts and that he was a US citizen, thus entitled to trial in the civil courts.

Circuit Judge Murrah, on behalf of the majority, dismissed the petition and held that the petitioner was an unlawful belligerent by use of the "traditionally recognized body of international common law" and that "the petitioner's citizenship in the United States does not divest the commission of jurisdiction over him, or confer upon him any constitutional rights not accorded any other belligerent under the law of war."[309]

3. Geneva Conventions

The Civilian Convention has not made any inroads into these decisions and the conclusion remains the same: the unlawful belligerent is not entitled to judicial review by the federal courts of his trial and conviction by the US military commission, irrespective of whether the trial took place within the United States or elsewhere.

Under the Article 3, GC standard of due process, there is no duty to permit the accused judicial review and none should be granted by the courts in absence of legislation.

4. Action by the Protecting Power

In addition to the review procedures within the military establishment and the remote possibility of securing judicial review

309.   Coplepaugh v Looney, 235 F. 2d 429 (10th Cir. 1956), cert. denied 325 U.S. 1014 (1956).

in a federal court, the unlawful belligerent is entitled to the services of a Protecting Power[310] or other humane organization to ensure that the Article 3 standard of due process is complied with by the Detaining Power.

When a denial of justice is asserted, the Protecting Power (a neutral or the ICRC) or the accused's state would seek to secure either a new trial or the release and repatriation of the unlawful belligerent, or modification of the sentence. Demand could also be made for those responsible to be tried for commission of a grave breach under the Civilian Convention.

The matter of disputes concerning the application of the Civilian Convention is provided for in Article 12 which requires the parties to submit their disagreement to the good offices of the Protecting Power and its proposals are to be given effect by the Parties, in hopes of prompt resolution of the matter. In the event the Protecting Power is unable to bring about a settlement, the Parties are urged to refer the matter to the International Court of Justice. A provision requiring compulsory submission to the World Court was rejected during the Diplomatic Conference of the 1949 Conventions because the United Nations Security Council was responsible for laying down conditions of the Court's jurisdiction

---

310. See COMMENTARY IV 80-92 for background on duties of the Protecting Power. See also, MacGildeon, Some Observations on the Part of Protest in International Law, 30 Brit. Yb. Int'l. L. 293 (1953), for general discussion on protests, a proper form of proceeding to remedy a claim of denial of justice.

under Article 35 of the Court's Statute.[311]

Brierly divides international disputes into two groups:
justiciable or those of a legal nature, and non-justiciable or
political nature.[312] Since we are dealing with judicial proceedings
under Article 3 of the Civilian Convention, all disputes would be
of a legal nature in which case they are referrable to the International Court of Justice as involving the interpretation of a treaty,
the question being whether vel non the granting or withholding of a
particular procedural right is in accord with the standard of
Article 3, namely, that sentences and executions follow the
judgment pronounced by a regularly constituted court, affording
all the judicial safeguards which are recognized as indispensable
by civilized peoples.[313]

---

311.   COMMENTARY IV 116-7. Where a death sentence is carried
out a wrongful damage claim might accompany the assertion of denial
of justice incident to that sentence. In such cases, the current
legislation prohibits payment of either personal injury or death
claims (10 USC § 2734, the Foreign Claims Act, and paragraph 8b,
Army Regulation 27-28, 20 May 1966). In the event of imprisonment
due to denial of justice, the same result would attach. Even
where the US acted contrary to international law, a foreign court
refrained from deciding the issue of liability. Falk, The
Shimado Case: A Legal Approach of the Atomic Attack Upon Hiroshima
and Nagasaki, 59 Am. J. Int'l. L. 759 (1965).

312.   LAW OF NATIONS 286 (5th ed 1961).

313.   Have the parties to the Geneva Conventions relinquished
any sovereign immunity from suit arising from denial of justice
claims? It is submitted that there has been no such relinquishment or waiver in the absence of an intent to do so. For general
discussion on topic, see Lauterpacht, The Problem of Jurisdictional
Immunities of Foreign States, 28 Brit. Yb. Int'l. L. 220, fn 237
(1951).

In the event of disputes regarding the trial of an unlawful belligerent, the proposals by the Protecting Power should be complied with as soon as rendered in order to maintain the humanitarian spirit of the Convention.

VIII

TRIAL OF THE UNLAWFUL BELLIGERENT IN OCCUPIED TERRITORY

A. Procedural Rights Before and During Trial

The third standard of procedural due process provided by the Geneva Conventions in the event of trial for war crimes is found in Articles 64-76 of the Civilian Convention.

Generally speaking, the Occupying Power is required to keep in effect all the local laws, consistent with its security. In the event new laws are enacted or local laws are modified, the Occupying Power must notify the people of the occupied territory and is not to try violations of such additions or modifications unless the accused had knowledge thereof. The Convention also provides for the local courts to continue during occupation, and that any laws enacted by the Occupying Power shall not have retroactive effect.[314] The Occupying Power's right to try persons for conduct violation of the law of war prior to occupation is clearly recognized in Article 70.

The Occupying Power is entitled to use only non-political military courts where the local courts are considered inappropriate, as would be the case with a war crime prosecution.[315] Most of the discussion in Section VII, dealing with the trial of the unlawful belligerent in non-occupied territory applies here, except as noted

---

314.   Art. 64 and 65, GC.

315.   Art. 66, GC.

below.

The Civilian Convention requires that the accused may be promptly informed of the charges against him in a language which he understands, and the right to a speedy trial. The Protecting Power (performing the same duties as under the Prisoner Convention) is to be notified three weeks in advance of trial but only in capital cases or where imprisonment can exceed two years. The Protecting Power is entitled to receive a copy of the file upon request. The Occupying Power is to provide the same information as in the case of a prisoner of war, except that the Civilian Convention calls for a citation of the penal law rather than a discussion of the applicable law. The appointing authority should, nevertheless, furnish the Protecting Power a copy of the pre-trial advice.[316]

The accused has the right to his choice of counsel and counsel is free to consult with his client and others and to have necessary facilities for defense. Where the accused fails to make a choice, the Protecting Power may do so. In a serious case, the Occupying Power is given the right to appoint counsel only where the accused failed to do so and the Protecting Power is not functioning.[317] The phrase "competent" interpreter in the Prisoner Convention is deleted and only an interpreter need be furnished; but the accused may waive the services of an interpreter at either the preliminary hearing phase or even during trial,

---

316.   Art. 71, GC.

317.   Art. 72, GC.

indicating a lessening of the concept of procedural process in these cases.[318] However, the record should clearly reflect the reasons for the waiver, especially in serious cases.

At trial, the accused has the right to present evidence, to call witnesses, and the assistance of counsel.[319]

Aside from the provisions dealing with procedural rights incident to a judicial proceeding, the Convention provides that where absolute military necessity so requires, a person otherwise protected by the Convention who is detained as a spy or saboteur or who is under "definite suspicion" of activity hostile to the security of the Occupying Power is considered as having forfeited his right to communicate.[320] Also, the Convention gives the Occupying Power great leeway in deciding what persons it can intern as control measures in the discharge of its duty to maintain law and order.[321] Hence, arrest and detention would be proper where there is more than mere suspicion that the accused committed the violation of the laws of war. Ex post facto laws

---

318.   Art. 72, GC.

319.   Ibid.

320.   Art. 5, GC. Article 25, GC gives the detained person the right to correspond with friends, relatives, etc. The International Commission of Jurists has studied the issue of detention and the right to communicate; recommend that even though a person can be detained in solitary confinement for maximum of twenty days in some states under emergency conditions, he should be allowed to contact his attorney. Report, The Right of Arrested Persons to Communicate, 85 (1964).

321.   Art. 41, GC.

are prohibited. There is no provision that requires the Occupying Power to conduct a pre-trial investigation.[322]

B. Sentencing Power

Considerable inroads have been made into the punishment which an Occupying Power can mete out for violations of the laws. Article 68 of the Convention limits the Occupying Power to impose the death sentence only where the offense involves espionage, serious acts against the military security of the Occupying Power, or intentional offenses resulting in death of one or more persons and further, that the death penalty must have been authorized under the law of the occupied country in force at the time the occupation commenced. The United States, in making one of its two reservations to the 1949 Geneva Conventions, reserved the right to impose the death penalty without regard to this last limitation. In explaining its reason, Messrs. Yingling and Ginnane state that the United States, joined by the United Kingdom, desired the ability to take drastic action against illegal combatants activities and thus be in a better position to protect itself.[323] It was the vote of those countries recently under occupation which, coupled with those nations which have abolished the death penalty, resulted in the Article 68 limitation. Pictet reports that the US wished to remain free to impose the death sentence in those situations

---

322.   Art. 85, GC.

323.   The Geneva Conventions of 1949, 46 Am. J. Int'l. L. 393, 424 (1952). The Reservation appears at 6 U.S.T. & O.I.A. 3694(1955).

where the soon-to-be-occupied country hastily abolished the death punishment.[324]

Another principle consideration is the distinction drawn by the Convention between major and minor offenses and the sanctions which can be imposed in each category. Internment or imprisonment for two years or less is required in the case of a minor offense which is defined as conduct not seriously damaging property of the Occupying Power or not constituting an attempt on life or limb of the forces of the Occupying Power.[325]

The attention of the court is to be invited to the fact that the protected person is not a national of the prosecuting State and that he is not bound to owe any allegience to it. The Convention also prohibits the imposition of the death penalty upon one not yet 18 years of age at the time of the offense.[326]

Details of the trial and sentence are to be forwarded to the Protecting Power where the death sentence or inprisonment for two years or more is imposed. Six months must elapse from the date of this notification until the execution of the death penalty. Sentences to imprisonment are to be served in the Occupied country, thus avoiding the mass transfer and deportations by Germany during the Second World War.[327] Upon liberation, these imprisoned personnel

---

324.   COMMENTARY IV 345-6.

325.   Art. 68, GC.

326.   Ibid.

327.   Art. 71, GC.

are to be handed over to the authorities of the liberated country.[328] As in the case of prisoners of war, time spent in pre-trial confinement is to be deducted from the approved sentence, and the sentence must be proportionate to the offense.[329]

C. Post-trial Procedural Matters

The Civilian Convention is silent as to the entitlement of procedural safeguards following trial, except that it provides in Article 66 that "Courts of appeal shall preferably sit in the occupied country." Although it is not clear from reading the reports of the Diplomatic Conference whether such courts were required, Mr. Pictet assumes that such courts are to consider the accused's case by way of an appeal.[330] Thus, the proceedings before the military commission of the unlawful belligerent would have to be revised, preferably by the War Crimes Modification Board, discussed in Section VII, sitting in the occupied country.

Similarily, the discussion on judicial review by the US courts contained in the above Section is applicable here.

In the Prisoner Convention, there was a provision relating to the resolving of disputes. Article 149 of the Civilian Convention provides similar machinery in the event there is a dispute between the interested Parties concerning a violation of

---

328.   Art. 77, GC.

329.   Art. 69, GC.

330.   COMMENTARY IV 340-1.

the Convention, as in the case of denial of justice. The inquiry procedure, originating in the 1929 Convention for Sick and Wounded in the Field, is obligitory when a Party to the Conflict requests it, although the method of procedure is left to the Parties. Also, Article 12 of the Civilian Convention provides for conciliation procedure, a feature common to all four Conventions, in order to resolve any disputes as quickly as possible and with the humanitarian purposes of the Conventions in mind.

IX

GRAVE BREACH PROSECUTIONS

A. Procedural Rights Before and During Trial

The fourth and last standard of a fair trial centers

around the Civilian Convention's grave breach article (Article 146)

which provides that a protected person, when charged with a grave

breach, is entitled to the "safeguards of proper trial and defense,

which shall not be less favourable than those provided by Article

105 and those following" of the 1949 Prisoner Convention. The

drafters considered that because most of the persons accused of grave

breach offenses would qualify under the expanded definition of a

prisoner of war (Article 4, GPW), it would be proper to provide

in the Civilian Convention that protected persons would also

benefit from certain Prisoner Convention safeguards.[331] However,

the emergence of the guerrilla fighter on today's scale apparently

was not contemplated by the drafters, although there was a manifesta-

tion of the new warfare raging in Greece, starting in 1947, in which

guerrillas carried on the effort of the Communists to bring about

the downfall of the Greek government.

Article 146 refers to four provisions of the Prisoner

Convention: Articles 105 through 108 which apply equally to the

unlawful belligerent captured incident to the conflict or on

occupied territory. These four GPW articles relate to qualified

---

331.   COMMENTARY IV 595.

defense counsel, two weeks to prepare for trial, (Art. 105) right
of petition or appeal (Art. 106, communication of details of the
sentence to the Protecting Power (Art. 107) and serving of sentences
in same establishments and same conditions as members of the
armed forces of the Detaining Power (Art 108).

Initially, the question is raised as to whether the Article
146 standard requires "identical" or "similar treatment" of the
protected person. There is no prohibition against the Detaining
or Occupying Power from granting to the protected person identical
treatment it accords to its armed forces personnel, but the intent
of the international community was not to assimilate the unlawful
belligerent into the penal provisions applicable to the military
forces of the prosecuting state, but merely to assure safeguards
which were not less favourable. First, the provisions of Article
105 will be discussed in this section, Article 107 and 108 in
Section B and Article 106, dealing with appeals, in Section C. Then,
an assessment in complying with these requirements will be made under
US practice.

Article 105 of the Prisoner of War Convention provides
these rights: assistance of qualified counsel of the accused's
choice and the assistance of a prisoner commrade; right to call
witnesses; services of a competent interpreter; procedure for the
selection of counsel should the PW or Protecting Power fail to
select within one; right of counsel to have two weeks to prepare
for trial; right of necessary facilities and freedom of interview
with the accused, other PW's, and any witness regarded by him as

necessary to interview; copy of the charges and allied papers to be furnished the PW and his counsel in a language which they understand; and a representative of the Protecting Power is entitled to attend the trial.

These rights enumerated in Article 105, GPW, appear in Articles 71 and 72 of the GC, and have been treated in this paper as being applicable in the trial under Article 3 standard of due process. Therefore, the unlawful belligerent on trial for committing a grave breach is to receive the same procedural safeguards as if he were tried under the Article 3 or the Articles 64-76 standards.

No mention, however, is made of the type or kind of court which shall conduct the trial of the grave breach prosecution. Article 146's reference to the Prisoner of War Convention does not have within its ambit any regard to a tribunal. Article 71, GC, does refer to a "regular trial" and Article 66 requires the Occupying Power to use its non-political military courts in the trial of inhabitants. Thus, the US military commission is the proper tribunal for the trial of the unlawful belligerent charged with a grave breach offense. The general court-martial's jurisdiction does not include this group of persons within its grant of authority and thus is not the proper tribunal.[332]

---

332.   Articles 104 and 106, UCMJ, (10 USC § 904 and 906) prescribe that any person charged with aiding the enemy or wartime espionage is subject to trial by either a court-martial or military commission. Because Article 2 of the UCMJ does not subject all persons to its provisions, the conclusion is forced that these two penal provisions are to be regarded as limited codification of the law of war and that only the military commission has jurisdiction to try those persons not subject to the Code.

B. Sentencing Power

Under Article 146, acting in a similar fashion to the due process clause of the 14th Amendment to the Constitution by applying standards to state government originally meant to apply only to the federal government,[333] the "protected person" is entitled to safeguards no less favorable than the sentencing power exercised by the Detaining Power in the case of prisoners of war. Article 107 of the Prisoner Convention deals with notification of findings and sentence to the Protecting Power and Article 108 concerns the execution of penalties.

As will be recalled from the Section involving prisoners of war, the Protecting Person is to be notified of the results of trial in a summary communication, indicating right of appeal, and whether the PW desires to appeal. Under the UCMJ, the PW is entitled to the benefits of the Table of Maximum Punishments, thus the convicted protected person would be entitled to a similar ceiling in the event punishment is imposed. Also, the form of punishment could not include confiscation, restoration of stolen property or indemnification, but would be limited to death, imprisonment or fine.

A detailed communication is to be forwarded the Protecting Power in the event the death sentence is adjudged by the military commission or in the event the sentence of any nature is ordered

---

333. See Brennan, Extension of the Bill of Rights to the States, 44 J. of Urban L. 11 (1966).

executed. This notification is to include a copy of the promulgating order, setting forth the offenses, the findings and sentence; a summarized report of the pre-trial investigation and trial; and location of place of confinement.

Article 108, GPW, requires that PW's serve their sentences "in the same establishments and under the same conditions as in the case of members of the armed forces of the Detaining Power." The Civilian Convention can be satisfied by according the convicted protected person with separate but equal facilities. There is no requirement that the protected person in this case be entitled to the _same_ benefits, just not less favourable. Had the drafters intended those convicted of grave breaches be entitled to the same provisions, such could have been provided. Here, the thrust of Article 146's reference to Articles 105 - 108 of the GPW is to the trial safeguards and appellate review. Other provisions dealing with confinement facilities are found in the Civilian Convention.

C. Post-Trial Procedural Matters

What appellate review is the protected person convicted of a grave breach entitled? Article 146, GC, provides for not less favourable treatment. Does this mean that the protected person is entitled to review of his conviction of a grave breach by the Board of Review, Court of Military Appeals, and Presidential action in the case of capital punishment? Or, is he entitled to a review procedure within the military as outlined in Section VII?

Article 106, GPW, provides that the PW "shall have, in the same manner as the members of the armed forces of the Detaining Power, the right of appeal or petition from any sentence pronounced upon him..." The PW is also to be advised of his right to appeal or petition and the applicable time limits in order to exercise this right.

A literal interpretation of Article 146 would compel the conclusion that the protected person is entitled to exactly the same review rights as the PW. But from a practical standpoint, it seems proper to conclude that "not less favourable" does not mean identical, thus the review within the military (first by the appointing authority and then the theater commander) is proper. Keeping in mind the purpose of trial - a fair and impartial hearing-, there appears to be little more to be gained by requiring all cases to be viewed by a procedure accorded by the US Army to its own personnel. It is untenable that a result reached under the literal interpretation would apply. None of the American delegation conveived of such a result during the drafting of the Conventions, nor is there mention of such a conclusion in the accounts following the signing in August 1949. In commenting on the application of this portion of the Civilian Convention, Mr. Yingling reports that Article 146 was designed to incorporate "roughly" some of the GPW provisions.

This area of the Conventions will provide a fertile field for controversy should the US deny an accused the same rights as enjoyed by a PW with regards to review procedure and grant the accused only the military review by the appointing and reviewing authority. It is submitted that the protected person is not entitled to a review of such porportions as the PW, since the purpose in both cases is to afford an opportunity to review the case, there being doubtful merit in the contention that there is more "justice" in a procedure having three or four levels of review than in one having one or two.

As discussed in Section VIII, regarding the trial of the inhabitant of occupied territory for war crimes, the protected person charged with a grave breach would be entitled to the Civilian Convention's provisions regarding conciliation and enquiry, so as to minimize disputes and ensure their prompt solution.

The "grave breach" trial would stand on the same footing as the trial under the Article 64-76 standard insofar as judicial review by US courts is concerned. It is regarded as improper for the US courts to review these proceedings in the absence of enabling Congressional legislation.

X.

CONCLUSIONS AND RECOMMENDATIONS

A. Conclusions

The questions propounded at the outset may now be answered.
The United States does have a duty under international law to
accord to the accused a fair trial on the basis of the 1949 Geneva
Conventions. The components of the concept of a "fair trial"
depend upon the status of the captive, the status of the captor and
the nature of the offense charged.

Where the accused charged with committing war crimes is
a prisoner of war, he is assimilated into the provisions of the
Uniform Code of Military Justice, irrespective of whether the US is
the Detaining Power or the Occupying Power. The "unlawful
belligerent", on the other hand, is to be tried according to
customary international law's concept of what constitutes a fair
trial when he is tried by a Detaining Power. At a minimum, these
procedural rights include: advance notice of the charges, assistance
of counsel and an interpreter, compulsory process to obtain witnesses
and other evidence, adequate time to prepare for trial, and a fair
and impartial tribunal before which the accused can present evidence
and cross-examine witnesses. The death sentence is possible in
such a trial. The "unlawful belligerent" tried for war crimes
committed during belligerent occupation and who qualifies as a
'protected person' is accorded due process under certain provisions
of the Geneva Civilian Convention which makes mandatory upon the

Occupying Power those rights just enumerated for the trial by the Detaining Power, plus: two weeks to prepare for trial, representative of the Protecting Power to be notified of the trial and attend the proceedings, instruction to the court that the accused owes no allegiance to the captor state, opportunity to appeal the findings and sentence, six month wait before execution of the death sentence, procedure for disputes as to application of the Convention, and no punishment in excess of two years for offenses not amounting to threat or loss of life or serious acts of sabotage against the Occupying Power.

The "fair trial" duty in the case of a non-PW for a grave breach includes those rights accorded the accused tried by the Occupying Power for a non-grave breach, plus additional procedural rights not less favorable than enjoyed by the PW when tried for war crime offenses. The effect of this last standard of a "fair trial" is to bring the accused in the non-occupied territory situation into the benefits conferred upon those tried by the Occupying Power. The rights of the unlawful belligerent tried by the Occupying Power already are not less favorable than the grave breach standard of procedural due process when tried by the United States.

The exercise of jurisdiction would be based on the territorial principle where the act took place in the United States or on territory over which the U.S. exercised exclusive control. The most frequent basis of jurisdiction over war criminals would be the universality principle, however.

The trial of the PW must be before a general court-martial

146

and appellate matters would follow the course now in effect for members of the U.S. armed forces, namely, review by a Board of Review and then the Court of Military Appeals in certain cases and approval by the President in the event of a death sentence. The military commission is the proper tribunal before which the unlawful belligerent is to be tried and the procedure attending such a trial is to be the same, irrespective of which of the three Civilian Conventions might apply, namely: assistance of counsel, adequate time to prepare for trial, services of an interpreter, right to call witnesses and introduce evidence, instruction to the tribunal that the accused owes no allegiance to the U.S., right to challenge the commission and the non-voting law member for cause, and review of the case by military authorities. The Protecting Power is to be advised of the proceedings and furnished all possible assistance and information.

Charges can be drawn from customary international law or from treaties and conventions in both the trial of the PW and the unlawful belligerent, except that capital cases are limited to the Table of Maximum Punishments in the case of the prisoner of war. Obtaining custody over the absent accused will depend for the most part on requesting his surrender from a military ally or on extradition treaties.

The right to select counsel should be limited only by security considerations in the case of both the PW and the unlawful belligerent. The introduction of evidence having probative value is proper in trials before the military commission, but is subject to technical exclusionary rules in trials before the general court-martial.

Compared with the WW II experience, future prosecutions, if any, would follow substantially the same procedure utilized by the United States in the conduct of its trials of war criminals before military commissions, except that the prisoners of war would be tried before a general court-martial and entitled to additional benefits accorded to members of the US Armed Forces under the Uniform Code of Military Justice.

B. Recommendations

At the present, there is absolutely no written guidance in the form of a directive or regulation regarding the manner in which a military commission will be created, operate, or its actions reviewed. To avoid the haphazard method of appointing these commissions as witnessed in World War II, there should be authorization to the commanders of the unified and specified commands to appoint such tribunals for the trial of war criminals, or to delegate this appointing authority one level.[334]

As to the operation and review of the commissions, the provisions of the Geneva Conventions set forth the standards of procedural due process incident to judicial proceedings, and our

334.   Such action would require amending paragraphs 30228 (unified commands) and 30247 (unified command) of Joint Chiefs of Staff Publication No. 2, Unified Action Armed Forces (Sep 1959), which set forth the present authority of these commanders.

WW II experience indicates that the United States will follow the granting of those rights which closely parallel the rights required of Articles 64 through 76 and Article 146, GC, irrespective of whether the Article 3 standard is applicable.

The need for additional treaties on the subject of extradition and for national legislation to implement the 1949 Geneva Conventions in the area of grave breaches has been examined and should provide the basis for action in order to ensure an effective system of repressing war crimes.

In closing, the war crimes trials conducted by the United States would follow two somewhat different procedures and before two different tribunals, depending on the status of the accused. Where the accused is a Prisoner of war, he will be tried before the general court-martial and subject to the procedural rights contained in the Uniform Code of Military Justice. The unlawful belligerent, however, would be amenable to trial before the military commission which would differ from the PW's trials in these procedural respects : no requirement for presence of accused at pre-trial investigation, no right to writ of habeas corpus in federal courts, (one evidentiary matter) no right to exclude hearsay evidence because of the probative value standard applicable in trials by the military commission, subject to death sentence for greater number of substantive offenses, and review of the findings and sentence will be conducted within the military system. In either event, the trial of the war criminal will accord the accused a "fair trial".